Sir Lewis Morris

Songs Unsung

Sir Lewis Morris

Songs Unsung

ISBN/EAN: 9783744753319

Printed in Europe, USA, Canada, Australia, Japan

Cover: Foto ©Thomas Meinert / pixelio.de

More available books at **www.hansebooks.com**

SONGS UNSUNG

BY

LEWIS MORRIS

OF PENBRYN

M.A.; HONORARY FELLOW OF JESUS COLLEGE, OXFORD
KNIGHT OF THE REDEEMER OF GREECE, ETC., ETC.

"FIDE ET AMORE"

FOURTH EDITION

LONDON

KEGAN PAUL, TRENCH & CO., 1, PATERNOSTER SQUARE

1884

PREFACE TO FOURTH EDITION.

THE writer has once more to express his acknowledgments for the great public favour with which this, his latest work, has been received since its appearance two months since.

In reply to strictures, which could hardly be meant seriously,* it may be well to say that the affix to the writer's name on his titlepage has no "territorial" significance whatever, but is simply an attempt to obviate to some extent the intolerable confusion arising from the identity of the writer's surname with that of an eminent contemporary writer of verse.

January 1st, 1884.

* *Saturday Review*, November 24th, 1883.

PREFACE.

AFTER a silence of more than three years, due to other engrossing occupations, the writer once more appeals to his readers with a volume in which the leading features of his former works will probably be found combined. The story of "Odatis" is derived from Athenæus. That of "Clytæmnestra in Paris" follows accurately, in all matters of fact, the evidence given in the well-known Fenayrou trial of August, 1882. The "Three Breton Poems" are from the "Barzaz Breiz." One of them, "The Foster Brother," has, as the author has learnt since his version was written, already appeared in a volume of Translations from the same source, published some years ago.

PENBRYN, CARMARTHEN,
October, 1883.

CONTENTS.

———∾———

SONGS UNSUNG.

PICTURES—I.

ABOVE the abysmal undivided deep
A train of glory streaming from afar ;
And in the van, to wake the worlds from sleep,
One on whose forehead shines the Morning-Star.

Long-rolling surges of a falling sea,
Smiting the sheer cliffs of an unknown shore ;
And by a fanged rock, swaying helplessly
A mast with broken cordage—nothing more.

Three peaks, one loftier, all in virgin white,
Poised high in cloudland when the day is done,
And on the mid-most, far above the night,
The rose-red of the long-departed sun.

———

A wild girl reeling, helpless, like to fall,
Down a hushed street at dawn in midsummer ;
And one who had clean forgot their past and all,
From a lit palace casement looks at her.

———

A young man, only clothed with youth's best bloom,
In mien and form an angel, not in eye ;
Hard by, a fell worm creeping from a tomb,
And one, wide-eyed, who cries, " The Enemy ! "

———

A lake of molten fires which swell and surge

And fall in thunders on the burning verge ;

And one a queen rapt, with illumined face,

Who doth defy the Goddess of the place.

Eros beneath a red-cupped tree, asleep,

And floating round him, like to cherubim,

Fair rosy laughter-dimpled loves, who peep

Upon the languid loosened limbs of him.

A darkling gateway, thronged with entering ghosts,

And a grave janitor, who seems to say :

" Woe, woe to youth, to life, which idly boasts ;

I am the End, and mine the appointed Way."

Songs Unsung.

A young Faun making music on a reed,
Deep in a leafy dell in Arcady :
Three girl-nymphs fair, in musing thought take heed
Of the strange youth's mysterious melody.

A flare of lamplight in a shameful place
Full of wild revel and unchecked offence,
And in the midst, one fresh scarce-sullied face,
Within her eyes, a dreadful innocence.

A quire of seraphs, chanting row on row,
With lute and viol and high trumpet notes ;
And, above all, their soft young eyes aglow—
Child angels, making laud from full clear throats.

Some, on a cliff at dawn, in agony ;
Below, a scaly horror on the sea,
Lashing the leaden surge.   Fast-bound, a maid
Waits on the verge, alone, but unafraid.

A poisonous, dead, sad sea-marsh, fringed with pines,
Thin-set with mouldering churches, old as Time ;
Beyond, on high, just touched with wintry rime,
The long chain of the autumnal Apennines.

A god-like Presence, beautiful as dawn,
Watching, upon an untrodden summit white,
The Earth's last day grow full, and fade in night ;
Then, with a sigh, the Presence is withdrawn.

A sheer rock-islet, frowning on the sea
Where no ship sails, nor ever life may be :
Thousands of leagues around, from pole to pole,
The unbounded lonely ocean-currents roll.

Young maids who wander on a flower-lit lawn,
In springtide of their lives as of the year ;
Meanwhile, unnoticed, swift, a thing of fear,
Across the sun, a deadly shadow drawn.

Slow, hopeless, overborne, without a word,
Two issuing, as if from Paradise ;
Behind them, stern, and with unpitying eyes,
Their former selves, wielding a two-edged sword.

A weary woman tricked with gold and gem,

Wearing some strange barbaric diadem,

Scorn on her lips, and, like a hidden fire,

Within her eyes cruel unslaked desire.

Two agèd figures, poor, and blurred with tears ;

Their child, a bold proud woman, sweeping by ;

A hard cold face, which pities not nor fears,

And all contempt and evil in her eye.

Around a harpsichord, a blue-eyed throng

Of long-dead children, rapt in sounds devout,

In some old grange, while on that silent song

The sabbath twilight fades, and stars come out.

The end of things created ; Dreadful night,

Advancing swift on sky, and earth, and sea ;

But at the zenith a departing light,

A soaring countless blessed company.

THE LESSON OF TIME.

LEAD thou me, Spirit of the World, and I
Will follow where thou leadest, willingly ;
Not with the careless sceptic's idle mood,
Nor blindly seeking some unreal good ;

For I have come, long since to that full day
Whose morning mists have fled and curled away—
That breathless afternoon-tide when the Sun
Halts, as it were, before his journey done,

Calm as a river broadening through the plain,
Which never plunges down the rocks again,
But, clearly mirrored in its tranquil deep,
Holds tower and spire and forest as in sleep.

How old and worn the metaphor appears,

Old as the tale of passing hopes and fears!

New as the springtide air, which day by day

Breathes on young lives, and speeds them on their way.

The Roman knew it, and the Hellene too;

Assyrian and Egyptian proved it true;

Who found for youth's young glory and its glow

Serener life, and calmer tides run slow.

And them oblivion takes, and those before,

Whose very name and race we know no more,

To whom, oh Spirit of the World and Man,

Thou didst reveal Thyself when Time began,—

They felt, as I, what none may understand;

They touched through darkness on a hidden hand;

They marked their hopes, their faiths, their longings fade,

And found a solitude themselves had made;

They came, as I, to hope which conquers doubt,

Though sun and moon and every star go out;

They ceased, while at their side a still voice said,

" Fear not, have courage ; blessed are the dead."

They were my brothers—of one blood with me,

As with the unborn myriads who shall be :

I am content to rise and fall as they ;

I watch the rising of the Perfect Day.

Lead thou me, Spirit, willing and content

To be, as thou wouldst have me, wholly spent.

I am thine own, I neither strive nor cry :

Stretch forth thy hand, I follow, silently.

VENDREDI SAINT.

THIS is Paris, the beautiful city,

Heaven's gate to the rich, to the poor without pity.

The clear sun shines on the fair town's graces,

And on the cold green of the shrunken river,

And the chill East blows, as 'twould blow for ever,

On the holiday groups with their shining faces.

For this is the one solemn day of the season,

When all the swift march of her gay unreason

Pauses a while, and a thin mask of sadness

Is spread o'er the features of riot and madness,

And the churches are crowded with devotees holy,

Rich and poor, saint and sinner, the great and the lowly.

    *   *   *   *   *   *

Here is a roofless palace, where gape

Casements in rows without form or shape :

A sordid ruin, whose swift decay

Speaks of that terrible morning in May

When the whole fair city was blood and fire,

And the black smoke of ruin rose higher and higher,

And through the still streets, 'neath the broad Spring sun,

Everywhere murder and rapine were done ;

Women lurking, with torch in hand,

Evil eyed, sullen, who soon should stand

Before the sharp bayonets, dripping with blood,

And be pierced through and through, or shot dead where

    they stood.

    *   *   *   *   *   *

This is the brand-new Hôtel de Ville,

Where six hundred wretches met death in the fire ;

Ringed round with a pitiless hedge of steel,

Not one might escape that swift vengeance.   To-day

The ruin, the carnage, are clean swept away ;

And the sumptuous façades, and the high roofs aspire,

And, upon the broad square, the white palace face

Looks down with a placid and meaningless grace,

Ignoring the bloodshed, the struggle, the sorrow,

The doom that has been, and that may be to-morrow,

The hidden hatred, the mad endeavour,

The strife that has been and shall be for ever.

*   *   *   *   *   *

Here rise the twin-towers of Notre Dame,

Through siege, and revolt, and ruin the same.

See the people in crowds pressing onward, slowly,

Along the dark aisles to the altar holy—

The altar, to-day, wrapt in mourning and gloom,

Since He whom they worship lies dead in the tomb.

There, by a tiny acolyte tended,

A round-checked child in his cassock white,

Lies the tortured figure to which are bended

The knees of the passers who gaze on the sight,

And the people fall prostrate, and kiss and mourn

The fair dead limbs which the nails have torn.

And the passionate music comes from the quire,

Full of soft chords of a yearning pity

The mournful voices accordant aspire

To the far-off gates of the Heavenly City;

And the soft clear alto, soaring high and higher,

Mounts now a surging fountain, now a heavenward fire.

Ay, eighteen centuries after the day,

A world-worn populace kneel and pray,

As they pass by and gaze on the limbs unbroken.

What symbol is this? of what yearnings the token?

What spell this that leads men a part to be
Of this old Judæan death-agony?

And I asked, Was it nought but a Nature Divine,
That for lower Natures consented to die?
Could a greater than human sacrifice,
Still make the tears spring to the world-worn eye?
One thought only it was that replied, and no other:
This man was our brother.

    *   *   *   *   *   *

As I pass from the church, in the cold East wind,
All its solemn teachings are left behind:
Here, once again, by the chill blue river,
The blighted buds on the branches shiver;
Here, again, are the holiday groups, with delight
Gaping in wonder at some new sight.

'Tis an open doorway, squalid and low,
And crowds which ceaselessly come and go.

Careless enough ere they see the sight
Which leaves the gay faces pallid and white :
Something is there which can change their mood,
And check the holiday flow of the blood.

For the face which they see is the face of Death.
Strange, such a thing as the ceasing of breath
Should work such miraculous change as here :
Turn the thing that we love, to a thing of fear ;
Transform the sordid, the low, the mean,
To a phantasm, pointing to Depths unseen.

There they lie, the dead, unclaimed and unknown,
Each on his narrow and sloping stone.
The chill water drips from each to the ground ;
No other movement is there, nor sound.
With the look which they wore when they came to die,
They gaze from blind eyes on the pitiless sky.

No woman to-day, thank Heaven, is here ;

But men, old for the most part, and broken quite,

Who, finding this sad world a place of fear,

Have leapt forth hopelessly into the night,

Bankrupt of faith, without love, unfriended,

Too tired of the comedy ere 'twas ended.

But here is one younger, whose ashy face

Bears some faint shadow of former grace.

What brought him here ? was it love's sharp fever ?

Was she worse than dead that he bore to leave her ?

Or was his young life, ere its summer came,

Burnt by Passion's whirlwinds as by a flame.

Was it Drink or Desire, or the die's sure shame,

Which led this poor wanderer to deep disgrace ?

Was it hopeless misfortune, unmixed with blame,

That laid him here dead, in this dreadful place ?

Ah Heaven, of these nineteen long centuries,

Is the sole fruit this thing with the sightless eyes !

Yesterday, passion and struggle and strife,

Hatreds, it may be, and anger-choked breath ;

Yesterday, fear and the burden of life ;

To-day, the cold ease and the calmness of death :

And that which strove and sinned and yielded there,

To-day in what hidden place of God's mysterious air ?

Whatever he has been, here now he lies,

Facing the stare of unpitying eyes.

I turn from the dank and dishonoured face,

To the fair dead Christ by his altar place,

And the same thought replies to my soul, and no other—

This, too, was our brother.

"NO MORE, NO MORE."

" No more, no more," the autumnal shadows cry;
" No more, no more," our failing hearts reply :
Oh ! that our lives were come to that calm shore
Where change is done, and fading is no more.

But should some mightier hand completion send,
And smooth life's stream unrippled to its end,
Our sated souls, filled with an aching pain,
Would yearn for waning days and years again.

Thrice blessèd be the salutary change
Which day by day brings thoughts and feelings strange !
Our gain is loss, we keep but what we give,
And only daily dying may we live.

THE NEW CREED.

Yesterday, to a girl I said—

" I take no pity for the unworthy dead,

The wicked, the unjust, the vile who die ;

'Twere better thus that they should rot and lie.

The sweet, the lovable, the just

Make holy dust ;

Elsewhere than on the earth

Shall come their second birth.

Until they go each to his destined place,

Whether it be to bliss or to disgrace,

'Tis well that both shall rest, and for a while be dead."

" There is nowhere else," she said.

" There is nowhere else."   And this was a girl's voice,

Who, some short tale of summers gone to-day,

Would carelessly rejoice,

As life's blithe springtide passed upon its way

And all youth's infinite hope and bloom

Shone round her ; nor might any shadow of gloom

Fall on her as she passed from flower to flower ;

Love sought her, with full dower

Of happy wedlock and young lives to rear ;

Nor shed her eyes a tear,

Save for some passing pity, fancy bred.

All good things were around her—riches, love,

All that the heart and mind can move,

The precious things of art, the undefiled

And innocent affection of a child.

Oh girl, who amid sunny ways dost tread,

What curse is this that blights that comely head ?

For right or wrong there is no further place than here,

No sanctities of hope, no chastening fear?

" There is nowhere else," she said.

" There is nowhere else," and in the wintry ground

When we have laid the darlings of our love—

The little lad with eyes of blue,

The little maid with curls of gold,

Or the belovèd agèd face

On which each passing year stamps a diviner grace—

That is the end of all, the narrow bound.

Why look our eyes above

To an unreal home which mortal never knew—

Fold the hands on the breast, the clay-cold fingers fold?

No waking comes there to the uncaring dead !

" There is nowhere else," she said.

Strange ; is it old or new, this deep distress?

Or do the generations, as they press

Onward for ever, onward still,

Finding no truth to fill

Their starving yearning souls, from year to year

Feign some new form of fear

To fright them, some new terror

Couched on the path of error,

Some cold and desolate word which, like a blow,

Forbids the current of their faith to flow,

Makes slow their pulse's eager beat,

And, chilling all their wonted heat,

Leaves them to darkling thoughts and dreads a prey,

Uncheered by dawning shaft or setting ray?

Ah, old it is, indeed, and nowise new.

This is the poison-growth that grew

In the old thinkers' fancy-haunted ground.

They, blinded by some keen too-vivid gleam

Of the Unseen, to which all things did seem

To shape themselves and tend,

Solved, by some Giant Force, the Mystery of Things,

And, soaring all too high on Fancy's wings,

Saw in dead matter both their Source and End.

They felt the self-same shock and pain

As I who hear these prattlings cold to-day.

Not otherwise of old the fool to his heart did say.

" There is no other place of joy or grief,

Nor wrong in doubt, nor merit in belief :

There is no God, nor Lord of quick and dead ;

There is nowhere else," they said.

And, indeed, if any to whom life's path were rough

Should say as you, he had cause maybe at sight.

For lo, the way is steep and hard enough,

And wrong is tangled and confused with right ;

And from all the world there goes a solemn sound

Of lamentations, rising from the ground,

Confused as that which shocks the wondering ear

Of one who, gliding on the still lagune,

Finds the oar's liquid plash and tune

Broken by wild cries of frenzy and of fear,

And knows the Isle of Madness drawing near ;

And the scheme of things, if scheme there be indeed,

Is a book deeper than our eyes may read,

Full of wild paradox, and vain endeavour,

And hopes and faiths which find completion never.

For such a one, in seasons of dismay

And deep depression and despair,

Clouds come ofttimes to veil the face of day,

And there is no ray left of all the beams of gold,

The glow, the radiance bright, the unclouded faith o

   old.

But you, poor child forlorn,

Ah ! better were it you were never born ;

Better that you had thrown your life away

On some coarse lump of clay;

Better defeat, disgrace, childlessness, all

That can a solitary life befall,

Than to have all things and yet be

Self-bound to dark despondency,

And self-tormented, beyond reach of doubt,

By some cold word that puts all yearnings out.

" There is nowhere else," she said :

This is the outcome of their crude Belief

Who are, beyond all rescue and relief,

Being self-slain and numbered with the dead.

" There is no God but Force,

Which, working always on its destined course,

Speeds on its way and knows no thought of change.

Within the germ the molecule fares free,

Holding the potency of what shall be ;

Within the little germ lurks the heaven-reaching tree :

No break is there in all the cosmic show.

What place is there, in all the Scheme Immense,

For a remote unworking Excellence

Which may not be perceived by any sense,

Which makes no humble blade of grass to grow,

Which adds no single link to things and thoughts we

 know ? "

" For everything that is, indeed,

Bears with it its own seed ;

It cannot change or cease and be no more :

For ever all things are even as they were before

Or if, by long degrees and slow,

More complex doth the organism grow,

It makes no break in the eternal plan ;

There is no gulf that yawns between the herb and

 man."

Poor child, what is it they have taught,

Who through deep glooms and desert wastes of thought

Have brought to such as you their dreary creed ?

Have they no care, indeed,

For all the glorious gains of man's long past,

For all our higher hope of what shall be at last ?

" All things are moulded in one mould ;

They spring, they are, they fade by one compulsion cold—

Some dark necessity we cannot know,

Which bids them wax and grow,—

That is sufficient cause for all things, quick and dead

" There is no Cause else," she said.

Oh, poor indeed, and in evil case,

Who shouldst be far from sound of doubt

As a maiden in some restful place

Whose busy life, year in year out,

Is made of gentle worship, homely days

Marked by their growing sum of prayer and praise,

The church spire pointing to the longed-for sky,

The heaven that opens to the cloistered eye.

For us, for us, who mid the weary strife

And jangling discords of our life

Are day by day opprest,

'Twere little wonder were our souls distrest,

God, and the life to be, and all our early trust

Being far from us expelled and thrust ;

But for you, child, who cannot know at all

To what hidden laws we stand or fall,

To what bad heights the wrong within may grow,

To what dark deeps the stream of hopeless lives may
    flow !

For let the doubter babble as he can,

There is no wit in man

Which can make Force rise higher still

Up to the heights of Will,—

No phase of Force which finite minds can know

Can self-determined grow,

And of itself elect what shall its essence be :

The same to all eternity,

Unchanged, unshaped, it goes upon its blinded way ;

Nor can all forces nor all laws

Bring ceasing to the scheme, nor any pause,

Nor shape it to the mould in which to be—

Form from the wingèd seed the myriad-branching tree,—

Nor guide the force once sped, so that it turn

To Water-floods that quench or Fires that burn,

Or now to the electric current change,

Or draw all things by some attraction strange.

Or in the brain of man, working unseen, sublime,

Transcend the narrow bounds of Space and Time.

Whence comes the innate Power which knows to guide

The force deflected so from side to side,

That not a barren line from whence to where

It goes upon its way through the unfettered air?

What sways the prisoned atom on its fruitful course?

Ah, it was more than Force

Which gave the Universe of things its form and face!

Force moving on its path through Time and Space

Would nought enclose, but leave all barren still.

A higher Power, it was, the worlds could form and fill;

And by some pre-existent harmony

Were all things made as Fate would have them be—

Fate, the ineffable Word of an Eternal Will.

All things that are or seem,

Whether we wake who see or do but dream,

Are of that Primal Will phantasms, if no more;

Who sees these right sees God, and seeing doth adore.

Joy, suffering, evil, good,

Whate'er our daily food,

Whate'er the mystery and paradox of things,

Low creeping thoughts and high imaginings.

The laughters of the world, the age-long groan,

Bring to his mind one name, one thought alone ;

All beauty, right, deformity, or wrong,

Sing to his ear one high unchanging song ;

And everything that is, to his rapt fancy brings

The hidden beat through space of the Eternal Wings.

Where did the Idea dwell,

At first, which was of all the germ and seed ?

Which worked from Discord order, from blind Force

Sped all the Cosmos on its upward course ?

Which held within the atom and the cell

The whole vast hidden Universe, sheltered well,

Till the hour came to unfold it, and the need ?

D

What did the ever-upward growth conceive,

Which from the obedient monad formed the herb, the tree.

The animal, the man, the high growths that shall be ?

Ever from simpler to more complex grown,

The long processions from a source unknown

Unfold themselves across the scene of life.

Oh blessed struggle and strife,

Fare onward to the end, since from a Source

Thou art, which doth transcend and doth determine Force !

Fare onward to the end ; not from Force, dead and blind

Thou comest, but from the depths of the Creative Mind.

Fare on to the end, but how should ending be,

If Will be in the Universe, and plan ?

Some higher thing shall be, that which to-day is Man.

Undying is each cosmic force :

Undying, but transformed, it runs its endless course

It cannot wane, or sink, or be no more.

Not even the dust and lime which clothe us round

Lose their own substance in the charnel-ground,

Or carried far upon the weltering wind ;

Only with other growths combined,

In some new whole they are for ever—

They are, and perish never.

The great suns shed themselves in heat and light

Upon the unfilled interstellar air,

Till all their scattered elements unite

And are replenished as before they were.

Nothing is lost, nor can be : change alone,

Unceasing, never done,

Shapes all the forms of things, and keeps them still

Obedient to the Unknown Perfect Will.

And shall the life that is the highest that we know,

Shall this, alone, no more increase, expand and grow ?

Nay, somewhere else there is, although we know not
    where,
Nor what new shape God gives our lives to wear.
We are content, whatever it shall be ;
Content, through all eternity,
To be whatever the Spirit of the World deem best ;—
Content to be at rest;
Content to work and fare through endless days ;
Content to spend ourselves in endless praise :
Nay, if it be the Will Divine,
Content to be, and through long lives to pine,
Far from the light which vivifies, the fire
Which breathes upon our being and doth inspire
All soaring thoughts and hopes which light our pathway
    here ;
Content, though with some natural thrill of fear,
To be purged through by age-long pain,
Till we resume our upward march again ;

Content, if need, to take some lower form,

Some humbler herb or worm

To be awhile, if e'er the eternal plan

Go back from higher to lower, from man to less than man.

Not so, indeed, we hold, but rather this—

That all Time gone, that all that was or is,

The scarpèd cliff, the illimitable Past,

This truth alone of all truths else hold fast :—

From lower to higher, from simple to complete.

This is the pathway of the Eternal Feet;

From earth to lichen, herb to flowering tree,

From cell to creeping worm, from man to what shall be.

This is the solemn lesson of all time,

This is the teaching of the voice sublime :

Eternal are the worlds, and all that them do fill ;

Eternal is the march of the Creative Will ;

Eternal is the life of man, and sun, and star ;

Ay, even though they fade a while, they are ;

And though they pause from shining, speed for ever still.

A GREAT GULF.

If any tender sire

Who sits girt round by loving faces

And happy childhood's thousand graces,

Through sudden crash or fire

Should 'scape from this poor life to some mysterious air,

And, dwelling solitary there,

Should feel his unfilled yearning father's heart

Pierced through by some intolerable smart;

And, sickening for the dear lost lives again,

Should through his overmastering pain

Break through the awful bounds the Eternal sets between

That which lives Here, and There, the Seen and the
      Unseen;

And having gained once more

This little Earth, should reach the scarce-left place

Which greets him with unchanged familiar face—

The well-remembered door,

The rose he watered blooming yet,

Nought to remember or forget,

No change in all the world except in him,

Nor there save in some sense already dim

Before the unchanged past, so that he seem

A mortal spirit still, and what was since, a dream ;

And in the well-known room

Should find the blithe remembered faces

Grown sad and blurred by recent traces

Of a new sorrow and gloom,

And when his soul to comfort them is fain

Finds his voice mute, his form unknown, unseen,

And thinks with irrepressible pain
Of all the happy days which late have been,
And feels his new life's inmost chambers stirred
If only of his own, he might be seen or heard ;

Then if, at length,
The father's yearning and o'erburdened soul
Burst into shape and voice which scorn control
Of its despairing strength,—
Ah Heaven ! ah pity for the present dread
Which rising, strikes the old affection dead !
Ah, better were it far than this thing to remain,
Voiceless, unseen, unloved, for ever and in pain !

So when a finer mind,
Knowing its old self swept by some weird change
And the old thought deceased, or else grown strange,
Turns to those left behind,

With passionate stress and mighty yearning stirred,—

It strives to stand revealed in shape and word

In vain ; or by strong travail visible grown,

Finds but a world estranged, and lives and dies alone !

ONE DAY.

One day, one day, our lives shall seem
Thin as a brief forgotten dream :
One day, our souls by life opprest,
Shall ask no other boon than rest.

And shall no hope nor longing come,
No memory of our former home,
No yearning for the loved, the dear
Dead lives that are no longer here?

If this be age, and age no more
Recall the hopes, the fears of yore,

The dear dead mother's accents mild,

The lisping of the little child,

Come, Death, and slay us ere the blood

Run slow, and turn our lives from good

For only in such memories we

Consent to linger and to be.

SEASONS.

THE cold winds rave on the icy river,
The leafless branches complain and shiver,
The snow clouds sweep on, to a dreary tune,—
Can these be the earth and the heavens of June ?—

When the blossoming trees gleam in virginal white,
And heaven's gate opens wide in the lucid night,
And there comes no sound on the perfumed air
But the passionate brown bird, carolling fair,

And the lush grass in upland and lowland stands deep,
And the loud landrail lulls the children to sleep,
And the white still road and the thick-leaved wood
Are haunted by fanciful solitude :

And by garden and lane men and maidens walk,
Busied with trivial, loverlike talk ;
And the white and the red rose, newly blown,
Open each, with a perfume and grace of its own.

The cold wind sweeps o'er the desolate hill,
The stream is bound fast and the wolds are chill ;
And by the dead flats, where the cold blasts moan,
A bent body wearily plods alone.

THE PATHOS OF ART.

Oft seeing the old painters' art,
We find the tear unbidden start,
And feel our full hearts closer grow
To the far days of long ago.

Not burning faith, or godlike pain,
Can thus our careless thought enchain ;
The heavenward gaze of souls sublime,
At once transcends, and conquers time.

Nor pictured form of seer or saint,
Which hands inspired delight to paint ;
Art's highest aims of hand or tongue,
Age not, but are for ever young.

But some imperfect trivial scene,

Of homely life which once has been,

Of youth, so soon to pass away,

Of happy childhood's briefer day;

Or humble daily tasks portrayed—

The thrifty mistress with her maid;

The flowers, upon the casement set,

Which in our Aprils blossom yet;

The long processions, never done;

The time-worn palace, scarce begun;

The gondolier, who plies his oar

For stately sirs or dames of yore;

The girl with fair hair morning-stirred,

Who swings the casement for her bird;

The hunt; the feast; the simple mirth

Which marks the marriage or the birth;

The burly forms, from side to side
Swift rolling on the frozen tide ;
The long-haired knights ; the ladies prim
The chanted madrigal or hymn ;

The opera, with its stately throng ;
The twilight church aisles stretching long
The spires upon the wooded wold ;
The dead pathetic life of old ;—

These all the musing mind can fill—
So dead, so past, so living still :
Oh dear dead lives, oh hands long gone,
Whose life, whose Art still lingers on !

IN THE STRAND.

In the midst of the busy and roaring Strand,
Dividing life's current on either hand,
A time-worn city church, sombre and grey,
Waits, while the multitude passes away.

Beside it, a strait plot of churchyard ground
Is fenced by a time-worn railing around ;
And within, like a pavement, the ground is spread
With the smooth worn stones of the nameless dead.

But here and there, in the spaces between,
When the slow Spring bursts, and the fields grow green,
Every year that comes, 'mid the graves of the dead
Some large-leaved flower-stem lifts up its head.

E

In the Spring, though as yet the sharp East be here,
This green stem burgeons forth year by year :
Through twenty swift summers and more, have I seen
This tender shoot rise from its sheath of green.

New busy crowds pass on with hurrying feet,
The young lives grow old and the old pass away ;
But unchanged, 'mid the graves, at the fated day,
The green sheath bursts upwards and grows complete.

From the grave it bursts forth, 'mid the graves it shall die,
It shall die as we die, as it lives we shall live ;
And this poor flower has stronger assurance to give,
Than volumes of learning, which blunder or lie.

For out of the dust and decay of the tomb,
It springs, the sun calling, to beauty and bloom ;
And amid the sad city, 'mid death and 'mid strife,
It preaches its mystical promise of life.

CŒLUM NON ANIMUM.

Oh fair to be, oh sweet to be
In fancy's shallop faring free,
With silken sail and fairy mast
To float till all the world be past!

Oh happy fortune, on and on
To wander far till care be gone,
Round beetling capes, to unknown seas,
Seeking the fair Hesperides!

But is there any land or sea
Where toil and trouble cease to be—
Some dim, unfound, diviner shore,
Where men may sin and mourn no more?

Ah, not the feeling, but the sky
We change, however far we fly ;
How swift soe'er our bark may speed,
Faster the blessed isles recede.

Nay, let us seek at home to find
Fit harvest for the brooding mind,
And find, since thus the world grows fair,
Duty and pleasure everywhere.

Oh well-worn road, oh homely way,
Where pace our footsteps, day by day,
The homestead and the church which bound
The tranquil seasons' circling round !

Ye hold experiences which reach
Depths which no change of skies can teach,
The saintly thought, the secret strife
Which guide, which do perturb our life.

NIOBE.

ON SIPYLUS.

Ah me, ah me! on this high mountain peak,

Which far above the seething Lydian plains

Takes the first dawn-shaft, and the sunset keeps

When all the fields grow dark—I, Niobe,

A mother's heart, hid in a form of stone,

Stand all day in the vengeful sun-god's eye,

Stand all night in the cold gaze of the moon,

Who both long ages since conspiring, slew

My children,—I a childless mother now

Who was most blest, a living woman still,

Bereft of all, and yet who cannot die.

Songs Unsung.

Ah day, ill-fated day, which wrecked my life !

I was the happy mother of strong sons,

Brave, beautiful, all in their bloom of age :

From him my first-born, now a bearded man,

Through the fair promise of imperfect youth,

To the slim stripling who had scarcely left

The women's chambers, on whose lip scant shade

Of budding manhood showed, I loved them all :

All with their father's eyes, and that strange charm

Of rhythmic grace, and musical utterance

As when, in far-off Thebes, the enchanted wall

Rose perfect, to the music of his lyre.

Ah me, the fatal day !   For at high noon

I sate within my Theban palace fair—

Deep summer-time it was—and marked the crowd

From the thronged city street, to the smooth plain,

Stream joyously: the brave youths, full of life,

Stripped for the mimic fray, the leap, the race,

The wrestling ; and the princes, my strong sons,

The fair limbs I had borne beneath my zone

Grown to full stature, such as maidens love,---

The sinewy arms, the broad chests, and strong loins

Of manhood ; the imperfect flower-like forms,

Eager with youth's first fires ; my youngest born,

My darling, doffing his ephebic robe

Which late he donned with pride, a child in heart,

In budding limbs a youth ;—I see them go

Their fair young bodies glistening in the sun,

Which kissed the shining olive.   As they went,

The joyous concourse winding towards the plain,

My happy eyes o'erflowed, and as I turned

And saw my daughters round me, fair grown lives

And virgin, sitting spinning the white flax,

Each with her distaff, beautiful and fit

To wed with any stately king of men

And reign a queen in Hellas, my glad heart

Broke forth in pride, and as I looked I thought,

" Oh happy, happy mother of such sons !

Oh happy, happy mother of such girls !

For whom full soon the joyous nuptial rites

Shall bring the expectant bridegroom and the bride,

And soon once more the little childish hands

Which shall renew my early wedded years,

When the king loved me first.   Thrice blest indeed.

There is no queen in Hellas such as I,

Dowered with such fair-grown offspring ; not a queen

Nor mother o'er all earth's plain, around which

flows

The wide salt stream of the surrounding sea,

As blest as I.   Nay, in Olympus' self

What offspring were they to all-ruling Zeus

That Leto bore?   Phœbus and Artemis,

A goodly pair indeed, but two alone.

Poor mother, that to such a lord as Zeus

Bare only those, no fairer than my own.

Nay, I am happier than a goddess' self ;

I would not give this goodly train of mine

For that scant birth.   I ask no boon of Zeus,

Nor of the Olympian Gods ; for I am glad.

No fruitful mother in a peasant's hut,

Scorning the childless great, thinks scorn of me,

Being such as I.   Nay, let Queen Leto's self

Know, that a mortal queen has chanced to bear

As fair as she, and more."

               Even as I spoke,

While the unholy pride flashed through my soul,

There pierced through the closed lattice one keen shaft

Of blinding sun, which on the opposite wall

Traced some mysterious sign, and on my mind

Such vague remorse and consciousness of ill,

That straightway all my pride was sunk and lost

In a great dread, nor could I longer bear

To look upon the fairness of my girls,

Who, seeing the vague trouble in my eyes,

Grew pale, and shuddered for no cause, and gazed

Chilled 'midst the blaze of sunlight.

　　　　　　　　　　　Then I sought

To laugh my fears away, as one who feels

Some great transgression weigh on him, some load

Which will not be removed, but bears him down,

Though none else knows it, pressing on his heart.

But when the half unuttered thought grew dim

And my fear with it, suddenly a cry

Rose from the city street, and then the sound

Of measured hurrying feet, and looking forth

To where the youth had passed so late, in joy,

Came two who carried tenderly, with tears,

A boy's slight form.   I had no need to look,

For all the mother rising in me knew

That 'twas my youngest born they bore ; I knew

What fate befell him—'twas the vengeful sun,

And I alone was guilty, I, his mother,

Who being filled with impious pride, had brought

Death to my innocent child.   I hurried down

The marble stair and met them as they came,

And laid him down, and kissed his lips and called

His name, yet knew that he was dead ; and all

His brothers stood regarding us with tears,

And would have soothed me with their loving words

Me guilty, who were guiltless, oh, my sons !

Till as I looked up from the corpse,—a cry

Of agony,—and then another fell

Struggling for life upon the earth, and then

Another, and another, till the last

Of all my stalwart boys, my life, my pride,

Lay dead upon the field, and the fierce sun

Frenzied my brain, and all distraught with woe
I to the palace tottered, while they bore
Slowly the comely corpses of my sons.

That day I dare not think of when they lay,
White shrouded, in the darkened palace rooms,
Like sculptured statues on a marble hearse.
How calm they looked and happy, my dear sons !
There was no look of pain within their eyes,
The dear dead eyes which I their mother closed ;
Me miserable ! I saw the priests approach,
And ministers of death ; I saw my girls
Flung weeping on the brothers whom they loved.
I saw it all as in a dream.   I know not
How often the dead night woke into day,
How often the hot day-time turned to night.
I did not shudder even to see the Sun
Which slew my sons ; but in the still, dead night,

When in that chill and lifeless place of death,

The cold, clear, cruel moonlight seemed to play

Upon the rangéd corpses, and to mock

My mother's heart, and throw on each a hue

Of swift corruption ere its time, I knew

Some secret terror lest the jealous gods

Might find some further dreadful vengeance still,

Taking what yet was left.

               At set of sun

The sad procession to the place of graves

Went with the rites of royal sepulture,

The high priest at its head, the nobles round

The fair white shrouded corpses, last of all

I went, the guilty one, my fair sweet girls

Clinging to me in tears; but I, I shed not

A single tear—grief dried the fount of tears,

I had shed all mine.

              Only o'ermastering fear

Held me of what might come.

                     When they were laid,

Oh, wretched me, my dear, my well-loved sons !

Within the kingly tomb, the dying sun

Had set, and in his stead the rising moon,

Behind some lofty mountain-peak concealed,

Filled all with ghastly twilight.   As we knelt,

The people all withdrawn a little space,

I and my daughters in that place of death,

I lifted up my suppliant voice, and they

With sweet girl voices pure, and soaring hymn,

To the great Powers above.

                   But when at last

I heard my hollow voice pleading alone

And all the others silent, then I looked,

And on the tomb the cold malignant moon,

Bursting with pale chill beams of light, revealed

My fair girls kneeling mute and motionless,

Their dead eyes turned to the unpitying orb,
Their white lips which should offer prayer no more.

Such vengeance wreaked Phœbus and Artemis
Upon a too proud mother.   But on me
Who only sinned no other punishment
They took, only the innocent lives I loved —
If any punishment, indeed, were more
Than this to one who had welcomed death.   I think
My children happier far in death than I
Who live to muse on these things.   When my girls
Were buried, I, my lonely palace gate
Leaving without a tear, sped hither in haste
To this high rock of Sipylus where erst
My father held his court; and here, long years,
Summer and winter, stay I, day and night
Gazing towards the far-off plain of Thebes,
Wherein I was so happy of old time,

Wherein I sinned and suffered.   Turned to stone
They thought me, and 'tis true the mother's heart
Which knows such grief as I knew, turns to stone.
And all her life ; and pitying Zeus, indeed,
Seeing my repentance, listened to my prayer
And left me seeming stone, but still the heart
Of the mother grows not hard, and year by year
When comes the summer with its cloudless skies,
And the high sun lights hill and plain by day,
And the moon, shining, silvers them by night,
My old grief, rising dew-like to my eyes,
Quickens my life with not unhappy tears,
And through my penitent and yearning heart
I feel once more the pulse of love and grief :
Love triumphing at last o'er Fate and Death,
Grief all divine and vindicating Love.

PICTURES—II.

A LURID sunset, red as blood,

Firing a sombre, haunted wood ;

And from the shadows, dark and fell,

One hurrying with the face of Hell.

———————

Two at a banquet board alone,

In dalliance, the feast being done.

And one behind the arras stands,

Grasping an axe with quivering hands.

———————

A high cliff-meadow lush with Spring ;

Gay butterflies upon the wing ;

F

Beneath, beyond, unbounded, free,
The foam-flecked, blue, pervading sea.

A clustering hill-town, climbing white
From the grey olives up the height,
And on the inland summits high
Thin waters spilt as from the sky.

A rain-swept moor at shut of day,
And by the dead unhappy way
A lonely child untended lies:
Against the West a wretch who flies.

Cold dawn, which flouts the abandoned hall
And one worn face, which loathes it all;

In his ringed hand a vial, while
The grey lips wear a ghastly smile.

Corinthian pillars fine, which stand
In moonlight on a desert sand ;
Others o'erthrown, in whose dark shade
Some fire-eyed brute its lair has made.

Mountainous clouds embattled high
Around a dark blue lake of sky ;
And from its clear depths, shining far,
The calm eye of the evening star.

A moonlight chequered avenue ;
Above, a starlit glimpse of blue :
Amid the shadows spread between,
The grey ghost of a woman seen.

A NIGHT IN NAPLES.

THIS is the one night in all the year
When the faithful of Naples who love their priest
May find their faith and their wealth increased ;
For just as the stroke of midnight is here,

Those who with faithful undoubting mind
Their " Aves " mutter, their rosaries tell,
They without doubt shall a recompence find ;
Yea, their faith indeed shall profit them well.

Therefore, to-night, in the hot thronged street
By San Gennaro's, the people devout,
With banner, and relic, and thurible meet,
With some sacred image to marshal them out.

For a few days hence, the great lottery
Of the sinful city declared will be,
And it may be that Aves and Paters said
Will bring some aid from the realms of the dead.

And so to the terrible place of the tomb
They go forth, a pitiful crowd, through the gloom,
To where all the dead of the city decay,
Waiting the trump of the judgment day.

For every day of the circling year
Brings its own sum of corruption here ;
Every day has its great pit, fed
With the dreadful heap of the shroudless dead.

And behind a grated rust-eaten door,
Marked each with their fated month and day,
The young and the old, who in life were poor,
Fester together and rot away.

Silence is there, the silence of death,

And in silence those poor pilgrims wearily pace,

And the wretched throng, pitiful, holding its breath,

Comes with shuffling steps to the dreadful place.

Till before these dark portals, the silent crowd

Breaks at length into passionate suffrages loud,

Waiting the flickering vapour thin,

Bred of the dreadful corruption within.

And here is a mother who kneels, not in woe,

By the vault where her child was flung months ago ;

And there is a strong man who peers with dry eyes

At the mouth of the gulph where his dead wife lies.

Till at last, to reward them, a faint blue fire,

Like the ghost of a soul, flickers here or there

At the gate of a vault, on the noisome air,

And the wretched throng has its low desire ;

And with many a praise of the favouring saint,

And curses if any refuses to heed,

Full of low hopes and of sordid greed,

To the town they file backward, weary and faint.

And a few days hence, the great lottery

Of the sinful city declared will be,

And a number thus shewn to those sordid eyes,

May, the saints being willing, attain the prize.

Wherefore to Saint and Madonna be said,

All praise and laud, and the faithful dead.

* * * * *

It was long, long ago, in far-off Judæa,

That they slew Him of old, whom these slay to-day ;

They slew Him of old, in far-off Judæa,—

It is long, long ago ; it was far, far away !

LIFE.

LIKE to a star, or to a fire,
Which ever brighter grown, or higher,
Doth shine forth fixed, or doth aspire ;

Or to a glance, or to a sigh ;
Or to a low wind whispering by,
Which scarce has risen ere it die ;

Or to a bird, whose rapid flight
Eludes the dazed observer's sight,
Or a stray shaft of glancing light,

That breaks upon the gathered gloom
Which veils some monumental tomb ;
Or some sweet Spring flowers' fleeting bloom ;—

Mixed part of reason, part belief,

Of pain and pleasure, joy and grief,

As changeful as the Spring, and brief ;—

A wave, a shadow, a breath, a strife,

With change on change for ever rife :—

This is the thing we know as life.

CRADLED IN MUSIC.

A BRIGHT young mother, day by day,
I meet upon the crowded way,
Who turns her dark eyes, deep and mild,
Upon her little sleeping child.

For on the organ laid asleep,
In childish slumbers light, yet deep,
Calmly the little infant lies ;
The long fair lashes veil its eyes.

There, o'er its childish slumbers sweet,
The winged hours pass with rapid feet ;
Far off the music seems to cheer
The child's accustomed drowsy ear.

Cradled in Music.

Hymn tune and song tune, grave and gay,
Float round him all the joyous day ;
And, half remembered, faintly seem
To mingle with his happy dream.

Poor child, o'er whose head all day long
Our dull hours slip by, winged with song ;
Who sleeps for half the tuneful day,
And wakes 'neath loving looks to play ;

Whose innocent eyes unconscious see
Nothing but mirth in misery.
The mother smiles, the sister stands
Smiling, the tambour in her hands.

And with the time of hard-earned rest,
'Tis his to press that kindly breast ;
Nor dream of all the toil, the pain,
The weary round begun again,—

The fruitless work, the blow, the curse,

The hunger, the contempt, or worse ;

The laws despite, the vague alarms,

Which pass not those protecting arms.

Only, as yet, 'tis his to know

The bright young faces all aglow,

As down the child-encumbered street

The music stirs the lightsome feet.

Only to crow and smile, as yet.

Soon shall come clouds, and cold, and wet ;

And where the green leaves whisper now,

The mad East flinging sleet and snow.

And if to childhood he shall come—

Childhood that knows not hearth or home,—

Coarse words maybe, and looks of guile,

Shall chase away that constant smile.

Cradled in Music.

Were it not better, child, than this,
The burden of full life to miss;
And now, while yet the time is May,
Amid the music pass away,

And leave these tuneless strains of wrong
For the immortal ceaseless song;
And change this vagrant life of earth
For the unchanged celestial birth;

And see, within those opened skies,
A vision of thy mother's eyes;
And hear those old strains, faint and dim,
Grown fine, within the eternal hymn?

Nay, whatsoe'er our thought may deem,
Not that is better which may seem;
'Twere better that thou camest to be,
If Fate so willed, in misery.

What shall be, shall be—that is all ;

To one great Will we stand and fall.

" The Scheme hath need "—we ask not why,

And in this faith we live and die.

ODATIS.

AN OLD LOVE-TALE.

CHARES of Mytilené, ages gone,
When the young Alexander's conquering star
Flamed on the wondering world, being indeed
The comrade of his arms, from the far East
Brought back this story of requited love.

——— ——— ———

A Prince there was of Media, next of blood
To the great King Hystaspes, fair of form
As brave of soul, who to his flower of age
Was come, but never yet had known the dart
Of Cypris, being but a soldier bold,
Too much by trenchèd camps and wars' alarms
Engrossed, to leave a thought for things of love.

Now, at this selfsame time, by Tanais

Omartes ruled, a just and puissant king.

No son was his, only one daughter fair,

Odatis, of whose beauty and whose worth

Fame filled the furthest East.   Only as yet,

Of all the suitors for her hand, came none

Who touched her maiden heart; but, fancy free,

She dwelt unwedded, lonely as a star.

Till one fair night in springtide, when the heart

Blossoms as does the earth, Cypris, the Queen,

Seeing that love is sweet for all to taste,

And pitying these loveless parted lives,

Deep in the sacred silence of the night,

From out the ivory gate sent down on them

A happy dream, so that the Prince had sight

Of fair Odatis in her diadem

And habit as she lived, and saw the charm

And treasure of her eyes, and knew her name

And country as it was; while to the maid

There came a like fair vision of the Prince

Leading to fight the embattled Median hosts,

Young, comely, brave, clad in his panoply

And pride of war, so strong, so fair, so true,

That straight, the virgin coldness of her soul

Melted beneath the vision, as the snow

In springtime at the kisses of the sun.

And when they twain awoke to common day

From that blest dream, still on their trancèd eyes

The selfsame vision lingered.   He a form

Lovelier than all his life had known, more pure

And precious than all words; she a strong soul

Yet tender, comely with the fire, the force

Of youthful manhood; saw both night and day.

Nor ever from their mutual hearts the form

Of that celestial vision waned nor grew

Faint with the daily stress of common life,

As do our mortal phantasies, but still

He, while the fiery legions clashed and broke,

Saw one sweet face above the flash of spears ;

She in high palace pomps, or household tasks,

Or 'mid the glittering courtier-crowded halls

Saw one brave ardent gaze, one manly form.

Now while in dreams of love these lovers lived

Who never met in waking hours, who knew not

Whether with unrequited love they burned, or whether

In mutual yearnings blest ; the King Omartes,

Grown anxious for his only girl, and knowing

How blest it is to love, would bid her choose

Whom she would wed, and summoning the maid,

With fatherly counsels pressed on her ; but she :

" Father, I am but young ; I prithee, ask not

That I should wed ; nay, rather let me live

My life within thy house. I cannot wed.

I can love only one, who is the Prince

Of Media, but I know not if indeed

His love is his to give, or if he know

My love for him ; only a heavenly vision,

Sent in the sacred silence of the night,

Revealed him to me as I know he is.

Wherefore, my father, though thy will be law,

Have pity on me ; let me love my love,

If not with recompense of love, alone ;

For I can love none else."

               Then the King said :

" Daughter, to me thy happiness is life,

And more ; but now, I pray thee, let my words

Sink deep within thy mind. Thou canst not know

If this strange vision through the gate of truth

Came or the gate of error.   Oftentimes

The gods send strong delusions to ensnare

Too credulous hearts.   Thou canst not know, in sooth,

If 'twas the Prince thou saw'st, or, were it he,

If love be his to give; and if it were,

I could not bear to lose thee, for indeed

I have no son to take my place, or pour

Libations on my tomb, and shouldst thou wed

A stranger, and be exiled from thy home,

What were my life to me?   Nay, daughter, dream

No more, but with some chieftain of my realm

Prepare thyself to wed.   With the new moon

A solemn banquet will I make, and bid

Whate'er of high descent and generous youth

Our country holds.   There shalt thou make thy choice

Of whom thou wilt, nor will I seek to bind

Thy unfettered will; only I fain would see thee

In happy wedlock bound, and feel the touch

Of childish hands again, and soothe my age

With sight of thy fair offspring round my knees."

Then she, because she loved her sire and fain

Would do his will, left him without a word,

Obedient to his hest; but day and night

The one unfading image of her dream

Filled all her longing sight, and day and night

The image of her Prince in all the pride

And bravery of battle shone on her.

Nor was there any strength in her to heal

The wound which love had made, by reasonings cold.

Or musing on the phantasies of love;

But still the fierce dart of the goddess burned

Within her soul, as when a stricken deer

O'er hill and dale escaping bears with her

The barb within her side; and oft alone

Within her secret chamber she would name

The name of him she loved, and oft by night,
When sleep had bound her fast, her pale lips formed
The syllables of his name.   Through the long hours,
Waking or sleeping, were her thoughts on him ;
So that the unfilled yearning long deferred
Made her heart sick, and like her heart, her form
Wasted, her fair cheek paled, and from her eyes
Looked out the silent suffering of her soul.

Now, when the day drew near which brought the feast,
One of her slaves, who loved her, chanced to hear
Her sweet voice wandering in dreams, and caught
The Prince's name ; and, being full of grief
And pity for her pain, and fain to aid
The gentle girl she loved, made haste to send
A messenger to seek the Prince and tell him
How he was loved, and when the feast should be,
And how the King would have his daughter wed.

But to the Princess would she breathe no word
Of what was done, till, almost on the eve
Of the great feast, seeing her wan and pale
And all unhappy, falling at her knees,
She, with a prayer for pardon, told her all.

But when the Princess heard her, virgin shame—
Love drawing her and Pride of Maidenhood
In opposite ways till all distraught was she—
Flushed her pale cheek, and lit her languid gaze.
Yet since she knew that loving thought alone
Prompted the deed, being soft and pitiful,
She bade her have no fear, and though at first
Unwilling, by degrees a newborn hope
Chased all her shame away, and once again
A long unwonted rose upon her cheek
Bloomed, and a light long vanished fired her eyes.

Meanwhile upon the plains in glorious war

The brave Prince led his conquering hosts; but

   still,

Amid the shock of battle and the crash

Of hostile spears, one vision filled his soul.

Amid the changes of the hard-fought day,

Throughout the weary watches of the night,

The dream, the happy dream, returned again.

Always the selfsame vision of a maid

Fairer than earthly, filled his eyes and took

The savour from the triumph, ay, and touched

The warrior's heart with an unwonted ruth,

So that he shrank as never yet before

From every day's monotony of blood,

And saw with unaccustomed pain the sum

Of death and woe, and hopeless shattered lives,

Because a softer influence touched his soul.

Till one night, on the day before the feast
Which King Omartes destined for his peers,
While now his legions swept their conquering way
A hundred leagues or more from Tanais,
There came the message from the slave, and he
Within his tent, after the well-fought day,
Resting with that fair image in his eyes,
Woke suddenly to know that he was loved.

Then, in a moment, putting from him sleep
And well-earned rest, he bade his charioteer
Yoke to his chariot three unbroken colts
Which lately o'er the endless Scythian plain
Careered, untamed ; and, through the sleeping camp,
Beneath the lucid aspect of the night,
He sped as speeds the wind. The great stars hung
Like lamps above the plain ; the great stars sank
And faded in the dawn ; the hot red sun

Leapt from the plain; noon faded into eve;

Again the same stars lit the lucid night;

And still, with scarce a pause, those fierce hoofs dashed

Across the curved plain onward, till he saw

Far off the well-lit palace casements gleam

Wherein his love was set.

                    Then instantly

He checked his panting team, the rapid wheels

Ceased, and his mail and royal garb he hid

Beneath a rich robe such as nobles use

By Tanais; and to the lighted hall

He passed alone, afoot, giving command

To him who drove, to await him at the gate.

Now, when the Prince drew near the vestibule,

The feast long time had sped, and all the guests

Had eaten and drunk their fill; and he unseen,

Through the close throng of serving men and maids

Around the door, like some belated guest

To some obscurer station slipped, and took

The wine-cup with the rest, who marvelled not

To see him come, nor knew him ; only she

Who sent the message whispered him a word :

" Have courage ; she is there, and cometh soon.

Be brave ; she loves thee only; watch and wait."

Even then the King Omartes, where he sate

On high among his nobles, gave command

To summon from her maiden chamber forth

The Princess. And obedient to the call,

Robed in pure white, clothed round with maiden shame,

Full of vague hope and tender yearning love,

To the high royal throne Odatis came.

And when the Prince beheld the maid, and saw

The wonder which so long had filled his soul—

His vision of the still night clothed with life

And breathing earthly air—and marked the heave

Of her white breast, and saw the tell-tale flush

Crimson her cheek with maiden modesty,

Scarce could his longing eager arms forbear

To clasp the virgin round, so fair she seemed.

But, being set far down from where the King

Sat high upon the daïs 'midst the crowd

Of eager emulous faces looking love,

None marked his passionate gaze, or stretched-forth hands;

Till came a pause, which hushed the deep-drawn sigh

Of admiration, as the jovial King,

Full tender of his girl, but flushed with wine,

Spake thus to her :

           " Daughter, to this high feast

Are bidden all the nobles of our land.

Now, therefore, since to wed is good, and life

To the unwedded woman seems a load

Which few may bear, and none desire, I prithee,

This jewelled chalice taking, mingle wine

As well thou knowest, and the honeyed draught

Give to some noble youth of those thou seest

Along the well-ranged tables, knowing well

That him to whom thou givest, thou shalt wed.

I fetter not thy choice, girl. I grow old ;

I have no son to share the weight of rule,

And fain would see thy children ere I die."

Then, with a kiss upon her blushing cheek,

He gave the maid the cup. The cressets' light

Fell on the jewelled chalice, which gave back

A thousand answering rays. Silent she stood

A moment, half in doubt, then down the file

Of close-ranked eager faces flushed with hope,

And eyes her beauty kindled more than wine,

Passed slow, a breathing statue. Her white robe

Among the purple and barbaric gold
Showed like the snowy plumage of a dove,
As down the hall, the cup within her hands,
She, now this way regarding and now that,
Passed, with a burning blush upon her cheek ;
And on each youthful noble her large eyes
Rested a moment only, icy cold,
Though many indeed were there, brave, fair to see,
Fit for a maiden's love ; but never at all
The one o'ermastering vision of her dream
Rose on her longing eyes, till hope itself
Grew faint, and, ere she gained the end, she turned
Sickening to where, along the opposite wall,
Sate other nobles young and brave as those,
But not the fated vision of her dream.

Meanwhile the Prince, who 'mid the close-set throng
Of humbler guests was hidden, saw her come

And turn ere she had marked him, and again

Down the long line of princely revellers

Pass slow as in a dream ; and all his soul

Grew sick with dread lest haply, seeing not

The one expected face, and being meek

And dutiful, and reverencing her sire,

She in despair might make some sudden choice

And leave him without love.   And as she went

He could not choose but gaze, as oft in sleep

Some dreadful vision chains us that we fail

To speak or move, though to be still is death.

And once he feared that she had looked on him

And passed, and once he thought he saw her pause

By some tall comely youth ; and then she reached

The opposite end, and as she turned her face

And came toward him again and where the jars

Of sweet wine stood for mingling, with a bound

His heart went out to her ; for now her cheek

Pale as the white moon sailing through the sky,

And the dead hope within her eyes, and pain

And hardly conquered tears, made sure his soul,

Knowing that she was his.

                But she, dear heart,

Being sick indeed with love, and in despair,

Yet reverencing her duty to her sire,

Turned half-distraught to fill the fated cup

And with it mar her life.

                But as she stood

Alone within the vestibule and poured

The sweet wine forth. slow, trembling, blind with tears.

A voice beside her whispered, " Love, I am here ! "

And looking round her, at her side she saw

A youthful mailèd form—the festal robe

Flung backward, and the face, the mouth, the eyes

Whereof the vision filled her night and day.

Then straight, without a word, with one deep sigh,

She held the wine-cup forth. He poured out first

Libation to the goddess, and the rest

Drained at a draught, and cast his arms round her,

And down the long-drawn sounding colonnade

Snatched her to where without, beneath the dawn,

The brave steeds waited and the charioteer.

His robe he round her threw; they saw the flare

Of torches at the gate; they heard the shouts

Of hot pursuit grow fainter; till at last,

In solitude, across the rounding plain

They flew through waking day, until they came

To Media, and were wed. And soon her sire,

Knowing their love, consented, and they lived

Long happy lives; such is the might of Love.

That is the tale the soldier from the East,

Chares of Mytilené, ages gone,

H

Told oftentimes at many a joyous feast

In Hellas ; and he said that all the folk

In Media loved it, and their painters limned

The story in the temples of their gods,

And in the stately palaces of kings,

Because they reverenced the might of Love.

IN WILD WALES.

I.

AT THE EISTEDDFOD.

THE close-ranked faces rise,
With their watching, eager eyes,
And the banners and the mottoes blaze above ;
And without, on either hand,
The eternal mountains stand,
And the salt sea river ebbs and flows again,
And through the thin-drawn bridge the wandering winds
    complain.

Here is the Congress met,
The bardic senate set,
And young hearts flutter at the voice of fate ;

All the fair August day

Song echoes, harpers play,

And on the unaccustomed ear the strange

Penillion rise and fall through change and counter-change.

Oh Mona, land of song !

Oh mother of Wales ! how long

From thy dear shores an exile have I been !

Still from thy lonely plains,

Ascend the old sweet strains,

And at the mine, or plough, or humble home,

The dreaming peasant hears diviner music come.

This innocent, peaceful strife,

This struggle to fuller life,

Is still the one delight of Cymric souls—

Swell, blended rhythms ! still

The gay pavilions fill.

Soar, oh young voices, resonant and fair ;

Still let the sheathed sword gleam above the bardic chair.

    *   *   *   *   *   *

The Menai ebbs and flows,

And the song-tide wanes and goes,

And the singers and the harp-players are dumb ;

The eternal mountains rise

Like a cloud upon the skies,

And my heart is full of joy for the songs that are still,

The deep sea and the soaring hills, and the steadfast

Omnipotent Will.

II.

AT THE MEETING FIELD.

Here is the complement of what I saw
    When late I sojourned in the halls of song,
The greater stronger Force, the higher Law,
    Of those which carry Cymric souls along.

No dim Cathedral's fretted aisles were there,
    No gay pavilion fair, with banners hung :
    The eloquent pleading voice, the deep hymns sung,
The bright sun, and the clear unfettered air,

These were the only ritual, this the fane,
    A poor fane doubtless and a feeble rite
    For those who find religion in dim light,
Strange vestments, incensed air, and blazoned pane.

But the rapt crowd, the reverent mute throng,

   When the vast listening semi-circle round,

Rang to the old man's voice serenely strong,

   Or swept along in stormy bursts of sound.

Where found we these in temples made with hands?

   Where the low moan which marks the awakened soul?

   Where, this rude eloquence whose strong waves roll

Deep waters, swift to bear their Lord's commands?

Where found we these? 'neath what high fretted dome?

   I know not.   I have knelt 'neath many, yet

Have heard few words so rapt and burning come,

   Nor marked so many eyes divinely wet,

As here I knew—"What will you do, oh friends,

   When life ebbs fast and the dim light is low,

When sunk in gloom the day of pleasure ends,

   And the night cometh, and your being runs slow,

And nought is left you of your revelries,

Your drunken days, your wantonness, your ill—

And lo ! the last dawn rises cold and chill,

And lo ! the lightning of All-seeing eyes,

What will you do ? "   And when the low voice ceased,

And from the gathered thousands surged the hymn,

Some strong power choked my voice, my eyes grew dim,

I knew that old man eloquent, a priest.

There is a consecration not of man,

Nor given by laid-on hands nor acted rite,

A priesthood fixed since the firm earth began,

A dedication to the eye of Light,

And this is of them.   What the form of creed

I care not, hardly the fair tongue I know,

But this I know that when the concourse freed

From that strong influence, went sedate and slow,

I thought when on the Galilean shore

    By the Great Priest the multitudes were led,

The bread of life, miraculously more,

    Sufficed for all who came, and they were fed.

SUFFRAGES.

" Surely," said a voice, " O Lord, Thy judgments
Are dreadful and hard to understand.

Thy laws which Thou madest, they withstand Thee,
They stand against Thee and Thy command :
Thy poor, they are with us evermore ;
They suffer terrible things and sore ;
They are starved, they are sick, they die,
And there is none to help or heed ;
They come with a great and bitter cry
They hardly dare to whisper, as they plead ;
And there is none to hear them, God or man;
And it is little indeed that all our pity can.

What, and shall I be moved to tears,

As I sit in this still chamber here alone,

By the pity of it,—the childish lives that groan,

The miseries and the sorrows, the hopes and the fears

Of this wonderful legend of life, that is one and the same

Though it differ in weal and in happiness, honour and

fame,—

Shall I turn, who am no more than a worm, to Thee,

From the pity of it—the want, the misery,

And with strong yearnings beat, and rebellions wild,

Seeing death written, and pain, in the face of a child ;—

And yet art Thou unmoved !

Ah, Lord, if Thou sawest surely!—and yet Thou dost see ;

And if Thou knewest indeed !—and yet all things are

clear to Thee.

For, Lord, of a truth Thy great ones,

Who have not their wealth of their own desert,

Live ever equal lives and sure,

And are never vexed nor suffer hurt,

But through long untroubled years endure

Until they join Thee, and are in bliss ;

Or, maybe, are carried away from Thee, and miss

Thy Face, which is too pure for them to see,

And are thenceforth in misery :

But, nevertheless, upon the earth

They come to neither sorrow nor dearth.

They are great, and they live out their lives, and Thou
        lettest them be ;

Thou dost not punish them here, if they despise

Thy poor and pass them by with averted eyes.

They are strong and mighty, and never in danger to fall ;

But Thou, Lord, art mighty and canst, and yet carest
        not at all.

But wherefore is it that such things are ;—

That want and famine, and blood and war

Are everywhere, and do prevail?

And wherefore is it the same monotonous tale

Is ever told by the lips of men ?

For there is hardly so hard a heart

In the breast of a man who has taken his part

In the world, and has little children around his knees,

But is filled with great love for them as Thou art for these,

And would give his life for their good, and is filled day
    and night

With fatherly thoughts of fear and yearning for right,

And grows sick, if evil come nigh them body or soul,

And yet is but a feeble thing, without strength or control.

But Thou art almighty for good; yet Thy plagues, they
    come,

Hunger and want and disease, in a terrible sum ;

And the poor fathers waste, and are stricken with slow
    decay;

And the children fall sick, and are starving, day after day ;

And the hospital wards are choked ; and the fire and the
    flood
Vex men still, and the leaguered cities are bathed in blood.

Ay, yet not the less, O Lord,
I know Thou art just and art good indeed.
This is it that doth perplex my thought,
So that I rest not content in any creed.
If I knew that Thou wert the Lord of Ill,
Then were I untouched still,
And, if I would, might worship at Thy shrine ;
Or if my mind might prove no Will Divine
Inspired the dull mechanical reign of Law.
But now, while Thou art surely, and art good,
And wouldst Thy creatures have in happiness,
Alway the sword, the plague prevail no less,
Not less, not less Thy laws are based in blood.
And such deep inequalities of lot
Confuse our thought, as if Thy hand were not.

All blessings, health and wealth and honours spent
On some unworthy sordid instrument ;
Thy highest gift of genius flung away
On some vile thing of meanest clay,
Who fouls the ingrate lips, touched with Thy fire,
With worse than common mire :
How should I fail alone, when all things groan,
To let my weak voice take a pleading tone !
How should I speak a comfortable word
When such things are, O Lord ! "

This is the cry that goes up for ever
To Heaven from weak and striving souls :
But the calm Voice makes answer to them never ;
The undelaying chariot onward rolls.

But another voice : " O Lord of all, I bless Thee,
I bless Thee and give thanks for all.

Thou hast kept me from my childhood up,

Thou hast not let me fall.

All the fair days of my youth

Thou wast beside, me and Thy truth.

I bless Thee that Thou didst withhold

The blight of fame, the curse of gold;

Because Thou hast spared my soul as yet,

Amid the wholesome toil of each swift day,

The tumult and the fret

Which carry worldly lives from Thee away.

I thank Thee for the sorrows Thou hast sent,

Being in all things content

To see in every loss a greater gain,

A joy in every pain;

The losses I have known, since still I know

Lives, hidden with Thee, are and grow.

I do not know, I cannot tell,

How it may be, yet death and pain are well:

I know that Thou art good and mild,

Though sickness take and break the helpless child ;

'Twas Thou, none else, that gav'st the mother's love,

And even her anguish came from Thee above.

I am content to be that which Thou wilt :

Tho' humble be my pathway and obscure,

Yet from all stain of guilt

Keep Thou me pure.

Or if Thy evil still awhile must find

Its seat within my mind,

Be it as Thou wilt, I am not afraid.

And for the world Thy hand has made,

Thy beautiful world, so wondrous fair :

Thy mysteries of dawn, Thy unclouded days ;

Thy mountains, soaring high through Thy pure air :

Thy glittering sea, sounding perpetual praise ;

Thy starlit skies, whence worlds unnumbered gaze ;

Thy earth, which in Thy bounteous summer-tide
Is clad in flowery robes and glorified ;
Thy still primeval forests, deeply stirred
By Thy great winds as by an unknown word ;
Thy fair, light-wingèd creatures, blithe and free ;
Thy dear brutes living, dying, silently :
Shall I from them no voice to praise Thee find ?
Thy praise is hymned by every balmy wind
That wanders o'er a wilderness of flowers ;
By every happy brute which asks not why,
But rears its brood and is content to die.
From Thee has come whatever good is ours ;—
The gift of love that doth exalt the race ;
The gift of childhood with its nameless grace ;
The gift of age which slow through ripe decay,
Like some fair fading sunset dies away ;
The gift of homes happy with honest wealth,
And fair lives flowering in unbroken health,—

All these are Thine, and the good gifts of brain,

Which to heights greater than the earth can gain,

And can our little minds project to Thee,

Through Infinite Space—across Eternity.

For these I praise Thy name ; but above all

The precious gifts Thy bounteous hand lets fall,

I praise Thee for the power to love the Right,

Though Wrong awhile show fairer to the sight ;

The power to sin, the dreadful power to choose

The evil portion and the good refuse ;

And last, when all the power of ill is spent,

The power to seek Thy face and to repent."

This is the answering cry that goes for ever

To Heaven from blest contented souls :

But the calm Voice makes answer to them never ;

The undelaying chariot onward rolls.

LOOK OUT, O LOVE.

Look out, O Love, across the sea :
A soft breeze fans the summer night,
The low waves murmur lovingly,
And lo ! the fitful beacon's light.

Some day perchance, when I am gone,
And muse by far-off tropic seas,
You may be gazing here alone,
On starlit waves and skies like these.

Or perhaps together, you and I,
Alone, enwrapt, no others by,
Shall watch again that fitful flame,
And know that we are not the same.

Look Out, O Love.

Or maybe we shall come no more,
But from some unreturning shore,
In dreams shall see that light again,
And hear that starlit sea complain.

SAINT CHRISTOPHER.

CHRISTOPHER !   There is many a name of Time
Higher than this in pride and empery;
There is a name which like a diadem
Sits on the imperial front, so that men still
Bow down to Cæsar ;—deathless names enough
Of bard and sage, soldier and king, which seize
Our thought, and in one moment bear us forth
Across the immemorial centuries
To Time's first dawns—a bright band set on high,
Who watch the surging of the restless sea
Whose waves are generations.   Yet not one
More strange and quaint and sweet than Christopher's,
Who bare the Christ.

In the expiring days
Of the old heathen ages lived the man
Who bore it first. The elder Pagan gods
Were paling now, and from the darkling groves
And hollow aisles of their resounding fanes
The thin shapes fled for ever. A new God
Awoke the souls of men ; and yet the shrines
Of Aphrodité and of Phœbus still
Drew their own votaries. The flower of faith,
Plucked from its roots, and thrown aside to die,
Is slow to wither, keeping some thin ghost
And counterfeit of fairness, though the life
Has fled for ever, and 'twas a dead thing
To which the Pagan bowed.
                              In the far East
He served, a soldier. Nature, which so oft
Is grudging of her blessings—mating now
The sluggish brain and stalwart form, and now

Upon the cripple's limbs setting the crown

Of godlike wisdom—gave with generous hand

Beauty and force to this one, mighty limbs

And giant strength, joined with the choicer gift

Of thoughts which soar, and will which dares, and high

Ambition which aspires and is fulfilled

In riches and in honour.

                Every year

Of prosperous manhood left him greater grown

And mightier.   Evermore the siren voice

Of high adventure called o'er land and sea ;

The magical voice, heard but by nobler souls,

Which dulls all lower music.   More than king

This great knight-errant showed ; a king of men

Who still before his strong eyes day and night

Saw power shining star-like on the hills,

And set his face to gain it.   Luxury

Held him nor sensual ease who was too great

For silken fetters, a strong soul and hand

Bent to a higher end than theirs, and touched

To higher issues ; a fair beacon set

Upon a lordly hill above the marsh

Of common life, but all the more laid bare

To the beating of the whirlwind.

                                    Every soul

Knows its particular weakness : so for him

This great strong soul set in its pride of place ;

The charm of Power worked like a spell ; high power

Unchecked, untrammelled, fixed with none to rule

Above it, this could bend the nobler soul

Which naught might conquer.   Over land and sea,

Hiring his mighty arm and strength, he fared

To sovereign after sovereign, always seeking

A stronger than the last : until at length

He found a puissant prince, so high, so great,

The strong sway held him, and he lived content

A sleeping soul, not knowing good or ill,

Resting in act, and with it satisfied—

A careless striving soul who sought no more.

But midst the miry ways of this sad world,

As now he fared unmoved, the frequent sight

Of evil ; the blind rage which takes and sways

The warrior after battle till he quench

His thirst in blood and torture ; the great pain

Which everywhere cries heavenward, every day

With unregarded suffrage ; the foul wrongs

Which are done on earth for ever ; the dark sins

Sinned and yet unrequited ; the great sum

And mystery of Evil, worked on him

Not to allure, not to repel, but only

With that strange spell of power which knows to take

The strong soul captive.   Here was power enough,

Mightier than mortal strength.   The greatest king

Whom ever he had served compared with this

Showed puny as a child ; this power which took

The mightiest in chains, now forcing them

To wrong and blood and ill, now binding them

With adamant chains within the sensual sty

Where they lay bound for ever.   Here was force

To limit Heaven itself.   So this strong soul

Bowed to it, taking Evil for his lord,

A voluntary thrall.   Yet not to him

The smooth foul ways of sense, the paths of wrong,

Brought pleasure of themselves ; only to know

The unrestrainèd passion surge, a beat

Of satisfied life, the glory and the glow

Of full untempered being.   And so long time

He served the Lord of Evil : deeds of wrong

And anger, deeds of soft and sensual sin,

All these he knew, a careless satisfied soul,

So that for dread of him men named his name

"The unrighteous;" but he cared not : power and fame

Sufficed him long, and hid from him the fashion

Of his own life and by what perilous ways

He walked, and by what fathomless black seas,

Abysmal deeps, and treacherous gulphs of Ill.

Till one day as they wandered (so the tale)

Through a thick wood whence came no gleam of light

To break the ghostly shadows —with amaze

He saw his master the great Lord of Ill

Cower down as from a blow and hide his eyes

From some white ghostly figure. As he gazed

The old chains fell from him, and with a glance

He rose up free for ever. For his soul

Met that great symbol of all sacrifice

Which men have worshipped since ; the soft sad eyes,

The agonised limbs nailed to the Tree of Death

Which is the Tree of Life ; and all the past

Fell from him, and the mystery of Love

And Death and Evil ; Might which gives itself

To liberate the world and dying breaks

The vanquished strength of Hell ; all these transformed

His very being, and straightway the strong soul,

Spurning his ancient chain, stood fair and free

Alone, a moment with the scars of gyves .

Upon his neck and limbs, and then fell down

Prostrate upon the earth, the mild eyes still

Bent on him pitiful.   There he lay stretched

Through the long night of sorrow, till at last

The sun rose on his soul, and on the earth,

And the pure dawn returning brought the day.

And when he rose the ancient mastery

And thirst for power, springing anew in him,

Once more, resistless, over land and sea

Impelled him, seeking this new mightier Lord

Who broke the power of Ill. So through all lands

He passed, a passionate pilgrim, but found not

The Prince he sought, only great princes, strong

And valorous he found, who bowed them down

Before the power of Evil ; but for them

He took no thought, who had seen their master blench

Before the Lord of Light ; but him indeed

He saw not yet ; filled with the pride of life,

A satisfied soul which bowed not down to wrong,

Touched with desire for good, since good was strong,

But loving strength alone.

     So as he fared

He came upon a dark and stony land

Where smiled no flower ; there, in a humble cell,

There dwelt an aged man ; no other thing

Of life was there, only wan age, which dwelt

Upon the brink of death. The giant strength

Was flagging now, while on the distant hills

The sun was sinking and the gray of night

Stole upward. Through the plain beneath the cell

A broad black river raged, where was no bridge

For travellers ; but a dark road stole to it

O'ergloomed by cypress, and no boat was there

Nor ferry, evermore beyond the shade

Breast-high the strong stream roared by black as
    death.

There sate he on the brink and saw no soul

As he gazed on the stream of death. Great misery

And weakness took him, and he laid him down

On that cold strand. Till, when his heart beat slow

And his life drooped, lo ! on the further shore

The sunset, lingering for a moment, fired

A thousand palace windows and the spires

And domes of a fair city ; then the night

Fell downward on them, but the unconquered soul

Within the failing body leaped and knew
That it had seen the city of the King.

Then swooned he for awhile, and when he knew
His life again he heard a reverend voice
Speak through the gloom.   And all the sun had set
And all the hills were hidden.

                              "Son, thou com'st
To seek the Lord of Life.   There is no way
But through yon cruel river.   Thou wert strong;
Take rest and thought till thy strength come to thee.
Arise, the dawn is near."

                              Then they twain went,
And there that sick soul rested many days.

And when the strong man's strength was come again,
His old guide led him forth to where the road
Sank in that black swift stream.   The hills were dark,

There was no city to see, nought but thick cloud,

And still that black flood roaring. Then he heard

The old voice whisper, "Not of strength alone

Come they who find the Master, but cast down

And weak and wandering. Oftentimes with feet

Wayworn and weary limbs, they come and pass

The deeps and are transformed ; but he who comes

Of his own strength from him long time the King

Hides him as erst from thee. Yet, because strength

Well used is a good gift, I bid thee plunge

In yon cold stream, and seek to wash from thee

The stains of life. No harm shall come to thee,

Nor in those chill dark waters shall thy feet

Slip, nor thy life be swallowed. It is thine

To bear in thy strong arms the fainting souls

Of pilgrims who press onward day and night

Seeking the Lord of Light. Thou, who so long

Didst serve the Lord of Evil, now shalt serve

K

A higher ; and because great penances
Are fitting for great wrong, here shalt thou toil
Long time till haply thou shalt lose the stain
Of sense and of the world, then shall thy eyes
See that thou wouldst.

                    Go suffer and be strong."

Then that strong soul, treading those stony ways,
Went down into the waters.   Painful souls
Cried to him from the brink ; sad lives, which now
Had reached their toilsome close ; worn wayfarers,
Who after lifelong strivings and great pain
And buffetings had gained the perilous stream
With heaven beyond ; wan age and budding youth
And childhood fallen untimely.   He stooped down
With wonder mixed with pity, raising up
The weakling limbs, and bearing in his arms
The heavy burden, through the chill dark depths

Saint Christopher.

Of those cold swirling waters without fear
Strode onward. Oftentimes the dreadful force
Of that resistless current, which had whelmed
A lower soul, bore on him ; oftentimes
The icy cold, too great for feebler hearts,
Assailed him, yet his mighty stature still
Strode upright through the deep to the far shore,
And those poor pilgrims with reviving souls
Blessed him, and left the waters and grew white
And glorified, and in their eyes he knew
A wonder and a rapture as they saw
The palace of the King, the domes, the spires,
The shining oriels sunlit into gold,
The white forms on the brink to welcome them,
And the clear heights, and the discovered heaven.

But never on his eyes for all his toil
That bright sun broke, nor those fair palace roofs

As erst upon his weakness.   Day and night
The selfsame cloud hung heavy on the hills,
Blotting the glorious vision.   Day and night
He laboured unrewarded, with no gleam
Of that eternal glory, which yet shone
Upon those fainting souls, whom his strong arms
Bore upward.   Day and night he laboured still,
Amid the depths of death.   Ay, he would rise
At midnight, when the cry of fainting souls
Called to him on the brink, and so go down
Without one thought of fear.   Yea, though the floods
Roared horribly, and deep called unto deep,
Through all those hidden depths he strode unmoved,
A strong, laborious, unrewarded soul.

Was it because the stain and blot of wrong
Were on him still uncleansed?   I cannot tell.
The stain of ill eats deep, and nought can cleanse it,

Nay hardly tears of blood.   But to my thought

Not thus the legend runs ; rather I deem

That what of good he loved was only strength,

The pride of conscious Power—that which had led him

To strong rude wrong, the same sense, working on him,

Led him through weariness of wrong to use

His strength for goodness.   Oftentimes Remorse

Comes not of hatred of the wrong, nor love

Of the good, but rather from the shame which Pride

Knows which has gone astray and spent itself

Upon unworthy ends.   So this strong soul

Laboured on unfulfilled.   Yet who shall trace

By what hidden processes of waste and pain

The great Will is fulfilled, and doth achieve

The victory of Good ?

                  So the slow years

Passed, till the giant strength at times would flag

A little, yet no feebleness was there,

But still the strong limbs carried him unmoved
Through those black depths of death.   Till one still
   night,
At midnight when the world was sunk in sleep,
The summons came, " A Pilgrim ! " and he saw
With a new-born compassion, on the shore
A childish form await him ; a soft smile
Was on the lips, a sweet sad glance divine
Within the eyes, as in a child's eyes oft
Knowledge not earthly, infinite weakness, strive
For mastery.   As the strong man stooped and took
The weakling to his breast, through the great might
Of Pity, grown to strength, he took the deep
With that light load in his arms.
                  But as he went,
The strength greater than human, the strong limbs
Which bore long time unfaltering the great pain
And burden of our life ; the fearless heart

Which never blenched before, though the winds beat

And all the night was blind ; these failed him now,

And as by some o'erwhelming load dragged down,

His flagging footsteps tottered ; the cold wave

Rose higher around him, the once mighty head

Bowed-down, the waters rising to his lip

Engulfed in the depths; the weight of all the earth

Seemed on his shoulders—all the sorrow, the sin,

The burden of the Race—and a great cry

Came from him, " Help ! I sink, I faint, I die,

I perish beneath my burden ! Help, O King

Of Heaven, for I am spent and can no more !

My strength is gone, the waters cover me,

I stand not of myself. Help, Lord and King !"

Then suddenly from his spent life he felt

The great load taken ; through the midnight gloom

There burst the glorious vision of his dream—

The palace of the King, the domes, the spires,

The shining oriels sunlit into gold,

The heaven of heavens discovered ; then a voice,

" Rise, Christopher ! thou hast found thy King, and
     turn

Back to the earth, for I have need of thee.

Thou hast sustained the whole world, bearing me

The Lord of Earth and Heaven.   Rise, turn awhile

To the old shore of Time ; I am the Prince

Thou seekest ; I a little child, the King

Of Earth and Heaven.   I have marked thy toils,

Labours, and sorrows ; I have seen thy sins,

Thy tears, and thy repentance.   Rise and be

My servant always.   And if thou shalt seek

A sign of me, I give this sign to thee :

Set thou thy staff to-night upon the verge

Of these dark waters, and with early dawn

Seek it, and thou shalt find it blossomed forth

Into such sweet white blooms as year by year
The resurrection of the springtide brings
To clothe the waste of winter.   This shall be
The sign of what has been."

                    And that strong soul,
Vanquished at length, obeyed, and with the dawn
Where stood his staff there sprung the perfumed cup
And petals of a lily : so the tale.
Nay, but it was the rude strength of his soul
Which blossomed into purity, and sprang
Into a higher self, beneath the gaze
Of a little child !   Nay, but it was the might
Of too great strength, which laid its robes of pride
Down on the ground, and stood, naked, erect,
Before its Lord, shamefast yet beautiful !
Nay, but it was the old self, stripped and purged
Of ingrained wrong, which from the stream of Death

Stood painful on the stable earth again,

And was regenerate through humility !

So for the remnant of his days he served

The Lord of Goodness ; a strong staff of right

Yet humble.   Till the Pagan Governor

Bade him deny the Prince who succoured him,

And he refusing, gained a martyr's crown

In cruel death, and is Saint Christopher !

PICTURES—III.

THE sad slow dawn of winter ; frozen trees
And trampled snow within a lonely wood ;
One shrouded form, which to the city flees ;
And one, a masquer, lying in his blood.

———— ——

A full sun blazing with unclouded day,
Till the bright waters mingle with the sky ;
And on the dazzling verge, uplifted high,
White sails mysterious slowly pass away.

————————

Hidden in a trackless and primæval wood,

Long-buried temples of an unknown race,

And one colossal idol ; on its face

A changeless sneer, blighting the solitude.

A fair girl half undraped, who blithely sings ;

Her white robe poised upon one budding breast ;

While at her side, invisible, unconfessed,

Love folds her with the shelter of his wings.

Black clouds embattled on a lurid sky,

And one keen flash, like an awakened soul,

Piercing the hidden depths, till momently

One seems to hear enormous thunders roll.

Two helpless girls upon a blazing wall,

The keen flames leaping always high and higher ;

But faster, faster than the hungry fire,

Brave hearts which climb to save them ere they fall.

A youthful martyr, looking to the skies

From rack and stake, from torment and disgrace ;

And suddenly heaven opened to his eyes,

A beckoning hand, a tender heavenly face.

A home on a fair English hill ; away

Stretch undulating plains, of gold and green,

With park and lake and glade, and homestead grey ;

And crowning all, the blue sea dimly seen.

A lifeless, voiceless, world of age-long snow,

Where the long winter creeps through endless night,

And safe within a low hut's speck of light,

Strong souls alert and hopeful, by the glow.

A great ship forging slowly from the shore,

And on the broad deck weeping figures bent ;

And on the gliding pierhead, sorrow-spent,

Those whom the voyagers shall see no more.

CONFESSION.

Who is there but at times has seen,
While his past days before him stand,
In all the chances which have been,
The guidance of a hidden Hand,

Which still has ruled his growing life,
Through weal and woe, through joy and pain,
Through fancied good, through useless strife,
And empty pleasure sought in vain ;

Which often has withheld the meed
He longed for once, with yearnings blind,
And given the truest prize indeed,
The harvest of a blessed mind ;

Songs Unsung.

And so has taken the common lot
Content, whate'er the Ruler would,
Since all that has been, or is not,
Springs from a hidden root of good?

     *   *   *   *

Yet some there are maybe to-day,
Whose childhood at the mother's knee
Was taught to bow itself and pray,
Nor ever thirsted to be free,

Who now, 'mid warring voices loud,
Have lost the faith they held before,
Nor through the jangling of the crowd
Can hear the earlier message more.

A brute Fate vexes them, the reign
Of dumb laws, speeding onward still,
Regardless of the waste and pain,
Which all the labouring earth do fill.

They look to see the rule of Right ;

They find it not, and in its stead

But slow survivals, born of Might,

And all the early Godhead dead ;

They see it not, and droop and faint

And are unhappy, doubting God ;

Yet every step their feet have trod

Was trodden before them by a saint.

*   *   *   *

Oh, doubting soul, look up, behold

The eternal heavens above thy head,

The solid earth beneath, its mould

Compacted of the unnumbered dead.

Here the eternal problems grow,

And with each day are solved and done,

When some spent life, like melting snow,

Breathes forth its essence to the sun.

L

As death is, life is—without end ;

Wrong with right mingles, joy with pain ;

Forbid two meeting streams to blend,

"Twere not more hopeless, nor more vain.

Though Death with Life, though Wrong with Right,

Are bound within the scheme of things,

Yet can our souls, on soaring wings,

Gain to a loftier purer height,

Where death is not, nor any life,

Nor right nor wrong, nor joy nor pain ;

But changeless Being, lacking strife,

Doth through all change, unchanged remain.

Should Wrong prevail o'er all the earth,

"Twere nought if only we discern

The one great truth, which if we learn,

All else beside is little worth.

Confession.

That Right, is that which must prevail,
If not here, there, if not now, then,
Is the one Truth which shall not fail,
For all the doubt and fears of men.

What if a myriad ages still
Of wrong and pain, of waste and blood,
Confuse our thought, triumphant Good
At length, at last, our souls can fill

With such assurance as the Voice
Which from the blazing mountain pealed,
And bade the kneeling hosts rejoice
That God was in His laws revealed.

Nay even might our thought conceive
The final victory of Ill,
Not so, were it folly to believe
That Right is higher, purer still.

Who knows the Eternal " Ought" knows well
That whoso loves and seeks the Right,
For him God shines with changeless light,
Ay, to the lowest deeps of Hell.

And whoso knoweth God indeed,
The fixed foundations of his creed
Know neither changing nor decay,
Though all creation pass away.

LOVE UNCHANGED.

My love, my love, if I were old,
My body bent, my blood grown cold,
With thin white hairs upon my brow,
Say wouldst thou think of me as now?
Wouldst thou cling to me still,
As down life's sloping hill
We came at last through the unresting years?
Art thou prepared for tears,
For time's sure-coming losses,
For life's despites and crosses,
  My love, my love?

Ah! brief our little, little day;
Ah! years that fleet so fast away;

Before our summer scarce begun,

Look, spring and blossom-tide are done !

When all things hasten past,

How should love only last ?

How should our souls alone unchanged remain ?—

Come pleasure or come pain,

In days of joy and gladness,

In years of grief and sadness,

    Love shall be love !

CLYTÆMNESTRA IN PARIS.

I SEEMED to pace the dreadful corridors

Of a still foreign prison, blank and white,

And in a bare and solitary cell

To find a lonely woman, soft of voice

And mild of eye, who never till life's end

Should pass those frowning gates. Methought I asked her

The story of her crime, and what hard fate

Left her, so gentle seeming, fettered there,

Hopeless, a murderess at whose very name

Men shuddered still. And to my questioning

Methought that dreadful soul made answer thus :

" Yes, I suppose I liked him. though I know not ;

I hardly know what love may be ; how should I ?--
I a young girl wedded without my will,
As is our custom here, to a man old,
Not perhaps in years, but dark experiences.
What had we two in common, that worn man,
And I, an untrained girl ?   It was not strange
If when that shallow boy, with his bold tongue,
And his gay eyes, and curls, and budding beard,
Flattered me, I was weak.   I think all women
Are weak sometimes, and overprone to love
When the man is young, and straight, and 'twas a triumph
To see the disappointed envious jades
Wince as he passed them carelessly, nor heeded
Their shallow wiles to trap him,—ay, a triumph !
And that was all ; I hardly know, indeed,
If it was love that drove, or only pride
To hold what others grudged me.   Vain he was,
And selfish, and a coward, as you shall hear

Handsome enough, I grant you, to betray
A stronger soul than mine.   Indeed, I think,
He never cared for me nor I for him
(For there were others after him) :   I knew it,
Then chiefest, when our comedy of life
Was turning at the last to tragedy.

"Now that I was unfaithful, a false wife,
I value not men's sneers at a pin's point,
We have a right to love and to be loved ;
Not the mere careless tolerance of the spouse
Who has none to give.   True, if I were a nun,
Vowed to a white and cloistered life, no doubt
'Twere otherwise.   They tell me there are women
Who are so rapt by thoughts of the poor, of churches,
Of public ends, of charity, of schools,
Of Heaven knows what, they live their lives untouched
By passion ; but for us, who are but women,

Not bred on moonlight, perhaps of common clay,

Untrained for aught but common bourgeois life,

Life is no mystical pale procession winding

Its way from the cradle to the grave, but rather

A thing of hot swift flushes, fierce delights,

Good eating, dances, wines, and all the rest,

When the occasion comes.   I never loved him,

I tell you ; therefore, perhaps, I did no sin.

" But when this fellow must presume to boast,

Grow cold, have scruples for his soul and mine,

And turn to other younger lives, and pass

My door to-day with this one, then with that,

And all the gossips of the quarter sneered,

And knew I was deserted, do you think it

A wonder that my eyes, opened at last,

Saw all the folly and the wickedness

(If sweet it were, where were the wickedness ?)

Which bore such bitter fruit?   Think you it strange

That I should turn for aid, ay, and revenge,

To my wronged spouse—if wronged he be, indeed,

Who doth consent as he did?   When I told him,

Amid my tears, he made but small pretence

Of jealousy at all; only his pride

Was perhaps a little wounded.   And indeed

It took such long confessions, such grave pain

Of soul, such agony of remorse of mine

To move him but a little, that I grew

So weary of it all, it almost checked

My penitence, and left me free to choose

Another for my love; but at the last,

Long labour, feigned reports, the neighbours' sneers,

These drove him at the last, good easy man,

To such a depth of hatred, that my task

Grew lighter, and my heart.

He bade me write

Loving appeals, recalling our past days
Together; and I wrote them, using all
The armoury of loving cozening words
With which craft arms us women : but in vain,
For whether some new love engrossed, or whether
He wearied of me and my love, I know not,
Only, in spite of all, no answer came.

"At length, since I could get no word from him,
My husband bade me write—or was it I
Who thought of the device?   Pray you believe me,
I would speak nothing else than the whole truth,
But these sad dreadful deeds confuse the brain.
Well, perhaps 'twas I, who knew his weakness well ;
I do not know, but somehow it came to pass
I wrote a crafty letter, begging of him,
By all our former kindness, former wrong,
If for the last time, recognizing well

That all was done between us evermore,

We might, for one last evening, meet and part.

And, knowing he was needy, and his greed,—

'If only he would come,' I wrote to him,

'I had some secret savings, and desired—

For what need comes there closer than a friend's ?—

To help him in his trouble.'

                    Swift there came—

The viper !—hypocritical words of love :

Yes, he would come, for the old love still lived,

He knew it, ah, too well ; not all the glamour

Of other eyes and lips could ever quench

The fire of that mad passion.   He would come,

Loving as ever, longing for the day.

"Now when we had the answer, straight we three—

My husband and myself, and his weak brother,

Whose daughter to her first communion went

That very day,—and I, too, took the Host

As earnest of changed life,—we three, I say,

At a little feast we made to celebrate

The brothers reconciled (in families

There come dissensions, as you know), devised

His punishment.   We hired, in a still suburb,

A cottage standing backward from the street,

Beyond an avenue of sycamores ;

A lonely place, unnoticed.   Day by day

We went, we three together—for I feared

Lest, if there were no third, the strength of youth

Might bear my husband down—we went to make

All needful preparations.   First we spread

Over all the floor a colour like to blood,

For deep's the stain of blood, and what shall cleanse it ?

Also, my husband, from a neighbouring wood,

Had brought a boar-trap, sharp with cruel knives

And jaggèd teeth, to close with a snap and tear

Clytæmnestra in Paris.

The wild beast caught within it. But I deemed
The risk too great, the prey might slip away ;
Therefore, that he might meet his punishment,
And to prevent the sound of cries and groans,
My husband fashioned for his lips a gag,
And on the mantel left it, and the means
To strike a light. And being thus prepared,
We three returned to Paris ; there long time
We sate eating and drinking of the best,
As those do who have taken a resolve
Whence no escape is, save to do and die.

" Then the two men went back and left me there,
With all my part to do. It was an hour
Or more before the time when my poor dupe
Had fixed to meet me. Wandering thus alone
Through the old streets, seeing the common sights
Of every day, the innocent child-faces

Homing from school, so like my little ones,

I seemed to lose all count of time.   At length,

Because it was the Ascension Feast, there came

A waft of music from the open doors

Of a near church, and, entering in, I found

The incensed air, all I remembered well—

The lights, the soaring chants, the kneeling crowds,

When I believed and knelt.   They seemed to soothe

My half bewildered fancy, and I thought—

What if a woman, who mayhap had sinned

But lightly, wishing to repair her wrong,

And bound thereby to some dark daring deed

Of peril, should come here, and kneel awhile,

And ask a blessing for the deed, of her

Who is Heaven's Queen and knows our weaknesses,

Being herself a woman !   So I knelt

In worship, and the soaring voices clear

And the dim heights and worship-laden air

Filled me with comfort for my soul, and nerved

My failing heart, and winged time's lagging flight,

Till lo the hour was come when I should go

To meet him for the last time.

                     " When we left

The city far behind, the sweet May night

Was falling on the quiet village street ;

There was a scent of hawthorn on the air

As we passed on with feint of loving words,—

Passed slow like lovers to the appointed place,

Passed to the place of punishment and doom

" But when we reached the darkling avenue

Of sycamores, which to the silent house

Led through a palpable gloom, I felt him shudder

With some blind vague presentiment of ill,

And he would go no further ; but I clung

                              M

Around him close, laughed all his fear to scorn,
Whispered words in his ear, and step by step,
My soul on reparation being set,
Drew him reluctant to the fated door
Where lay my spouse in ambush, and swift death.

"I think I hear the dreadful noise of the key,
Turning within the disused lock, the hall
Breathing a false desertion, the loud sound
Of both our footsteps echoing through the house.
I could not choose but tremble. Yet I knew
'Twas but a foolish weakness. Then I struck
A match, and in the burst of sudden light
I saw the ruddy cheek grown ashy pale,
And as he doffed his hat, I marked the curls
On his white forehead, and the boyish grace
Which hung around him still, and almost felt
Compassion. Then the darkness came again.

And hid him, and I groped to find his hand,
Clutched it with mine, and led him to the door.

" But when within the darkling room we were
Where swift death waited him, not dalliance,
Three times my trembling fingers failed to wake
The twinkling light which scarce could pierce the gloom
Which hid my husband.   Oh, to see his face
When the dark aspect and the furious eyes
Glared out on him ! ' I am lost !' he cried, ' I am lost !'
And then the sound of swift and desperate fight
And a death struggle.   Listening, as I stood
Without, with that mean craven hound, our brother,
I heard low cries of rage, and knew despair
And youth had nerved the unarmed in such sort
As made the conflict doubtful.   Then I rushed
Between them, threw my arms around him, clogged
His force and held him fast, crying the while,

' Wretch, would you kill my husband !'—held him fast,

As coils a serpent round the escaping deer,

Until my husband, hissing forth his hate,

' Villain, I pierce thy heart as thou hast mine,'

Stabbed through and through his heart.

" But oh, but oh

The lonely road, beneath the dreadful stars !

To the swift stream, we three—nay, nay, we four—

One on the child's poor carriage covered o'er,

And three who drew him onward, on the road,

That dead thing, having neither eye nor ear,

Which late was full of life, and strife, and hate.

On that dumb silence, came no wayfarer,

And once the covering which concealed our load

Slipped down, and left the ghastly blood-stained thing

Open to prying eyes, but none were there ;

And then the darkling river, and the sound

When, with lead coiled around it, the dead corpse

Sank with a sullen plunge within the deep,

And took with it the tokens of our crime.

" Then with a something of relief, as those

Who have passed through some great peril all unharmed,

We went and burned the blood-stained signs of death,

And left the dreadful place, and once more sped

To Paris and to sleep, till the new day,

Now risen to high noon, touched our sad dreams.

" And that day, since we could not work as yet,

We to the Picture Gallery went, and there

We took our fill of nude voluptuous limbs,

Mingled with scenes of horror bathed in blood,

Such as our painters love. So week by week,

Careless and unafraid, we spent our days,

Till when that sad night faded; swift there rose,

Bursting the weights that kept it, the pale corpse,
A damning witness from the deep, and brought
The dreadful past again, and with it doom.

" You know how we were tried, and how things went,
The cozening speeches, the brow-beating judge,
The petty crafts which make the pleader's art,
The dolts who sit in judgment, when the one
Who knows all must be silent ; but you know not
The intolerable burden of suspense,
The hard and hateful gaze of hungry eyes
Which gloat upon your suffering.   When doom came
It was well to know the worst, and hear no more
The half-forgotten horrors.   But I think
The sense of common peril, common wrong,
Knits us in indissoluble unity,
Closer than years of converse.   When my husband,
Braving his doom, embraced me as he went :

' Wife, so thou live I care not,' all my heart
Went out to him for a moment, and I cried,
' Let me die too, my guilt is more than his.'

" Some quibble marred the sentence, and once more
The miserable tale was told afresh :
Once more I stood before those hungry eyes,
And when 'twas done we went forth slaves for life,
Both with an equal doom, and ever since
We suffer the same pains in solitude,
Slaves fettered fast, whom only death sets free.

" That is my tale told truly. Now you know,
Sir, of what fashion I am made : a woman
Gentle, you see, and mild eyed. If I sinned
Surely there was temptation, and I sought
Such reparation as I could. There are here
Tigresses, and not women, black of brow

And strong of arm, who have struck down or stabbed

Husband, or child, or lover, not as I,

But driven by rage and jealousy, and drink !

These creatures of the devil, as I pass

I see them shrink and shudder.   The young priest

Of the prison, a well-favoured lad he is,

When I confessed to him bore on his brow

Cold drops of agony ; the Sister grew

So pale at what I told her, that I thought

She was like to swoon away, until I soothed her.

Poor wretch, she has much to learn ; and here I am,

And shall be till my hair turns grey, my eyes

Grow dim, and I have clean forgotten all

That brought me here, and all my former life

Fades like a once-heard tale.   In the long nights,

As I lie alone in my cell like any nun,

I wake sometimes with a start, and seem to hear

That rusty lock turn, and those echoing feet

Down that dark passage, and I seem to see

The dreadful stare of those despairing eyes,

And then there sounds, a plunge in the deep, and I

Lie shivering till the dawn.   I have no comfort

Except the holy Mass ; for see you, sir,

I was devout until they scoffed at me.

And now I know there is a hell indeed,

Since this place is on earth.   I do not think

I have much cause to fear death, should it come ;

For whoso strives for Duty, all the Saints

And the Madonna needs must love, and I,

I have done what penitence could do ; and here

What have I of reward ?—my children taken

As clean from me as if they were dead indeed,

Trained to forget their mother.   Sir, I see,

Beyond these shallow phantasms of life ;

And this I hold, that one whose conscience shows

As clear as mine must needs be justified.

I love the holy Mass, and take the Host

As often as I may, being of good heart.

For what was it she did in Holy Writ,

The Kenite's wife of old ?   I do not read

That women shrunk from her because she drave

The nail through her guest's brain ; nay, rather, praise

Was hers : yet was she not betrayed as I,

Nor yet repentant of her wrong and seeking

To do what good was left.   But look you, sir,

If I was once repentant, that is past :

I hate those black-browed women, who turn from me,

That smooth priest and that poor fool with her cross,

And that strange pink-and-whiteness of the nun.

And sometimes when they come I let them hear

Such things as make the pious hypocrites turn

And cross themselves.   And for this tigress crew,

If I might only steal to their cells at night

With a knife, I would teach them, what it is to stab ;

Or even without one, that these little hands
Can strangle with the best.

                    Ah, you draw back,
You too are shocked forsooth.   Listen, you wretch,
Who are walking free while I am prisoned here :
How many thoughts of murder have you nursed
Within your miserable heart ! how many
Low, foul desires which would degrade the brute !
Do you think I do not know you men ?   What was it
That kept your hands unstained, but accident ?—
Accident, did I say ? or was it rather
Cowardice, that you feared the stripes of the law,
And did not dare to do your will or die ?—
Accident ! then, I pray you, where the merit
To have abstained ?   Or if you claim, indeed,
Such precious self-restraint as keeps your feet
From straying, where the credit ? since it came
A gift as much unearned as other's ill,

Which lurked for them a little tiny speck

Hidden in the convolutions of the brain,

To grow with their growth, and wax with their years, and
   leave

The wretch at last in Hell.   Do you deem it just,

The Potter with our clay upon His wheel

Should shape it in such form?   I love not God,

Being such ; I hate Him rather : I, His creature,

I do impugn His justice or His power,

I will not feign obedience—I, a woman,

Of a soft nature, who would love my love,

And my child, and nothing more ; who am, instead,

A murderess, as they tell me, pining here

In hell before my time."

                    Even as she spake

I seemed to be again as when I saw

The murderess of old time ; and once again

Within this modern prison, blank and white,

There came the viewless trouble in the air

Which took her, and the sweep of wings unseen,

And terrible sounds which swooped on her and hushed

Her voice and seemed to occupy her soul

With horror and despair; and as I passed

The crucifix within the corridor,

" How long?" I cried, " How long?"

AT THE END.

When the five gateways of the soul
Are closing one by one,
When our being's currents slowly roll
And life nigh done,
What shall our chiefest comfort be
Amid this misery ?

Not to have stores heaped up on high
Of gold and precious things,
Not to have flown from sky to sky
On Fame's wide wings, —
All these things for a space do last,
And then are overpast.

Nor to have worked with patient brain

In senate or in mart,

To have gained the meed which those attain

Who have played their part,—

Effort is fair, success is sweet,

But leave life incomplete.

Nor to have said, as the fool said,

" Be merry, soul, rejoice ;

" Thou hast laid up store for many days."

Oh, foolish voice !

Already at thy gate the feet

Of the corpse-bearers meet.

Nor to have heaped up precious store

Of all the gains of time,

Of long-dead sages' treasured lore,

Or deathless rhyme,—

Songs Unsung.

Learning's a sweet and comely maid,
But Death makes her afraid.

Nor to have drained the cup of youth,
To the sweet maddening lees ;
Nor, rapt by dreams of Hidden Truth,
To have spurned all these ;—
Pleasure, Denial, touch not him
Whose body and mind are dim.

Not one of all these things shall I
For comfort use, or strength,
When the sure hour, when I shall die,
Takes me at length ;
One thought alone shall bring redress
For that great heaviness :—

At the End.

That I have held each struggling soul

As of one kin and blood,

That one sure link doth all control

To one close brotherhood ;

For who the race of men doth love,

Loves also Him above.

THREE BRETON POEMS.

I.

THE ORPHAN GIRL OF LANNION.

IN seventeen hundred and eighty-three,
To Lannion came dole and misery.

Mignon an orphan, as good as fair,
Served in the little hostelry there.

One darkling night, when the hour was late,
Two travellers rang at the outer gate.

" Quick, hostess ! supper, red wine, and food ;
We have money to pay, so that all be good."

When they had drunken enough, and more,
" Here is white money to pay the score.

" And now shall your little serving-maid come,
With her lantern lighted, to guide us home."

" Gentles, in all our wide Brittany
There is no man would harm her so let it be."

Forth went the maid, full of innocent pride,
Fearless and free, with her light by her side.

     *   *   *   *

When they were far on their lonely way,
They began to whisper, and mutter, and say,

" Little maid, your face is as fair and bright
As the foam on the wave in the morning light."

" Gentles, I pray you, flatter me not :
It is as God made it—no other, God wot ;

" And were it fairer, I tell you true—
Ay, a hundred times fairer—'twere nought to you."

" To judge, little maid, by your sober speech,
You know all the good priests at the school can teach ;

" To judge from your accents, discreet and mild,
You were bred in the convent cloister, my child."

" No teacher had I, neither priest nor nun ;
There was no one to teach me on earth, not one.

" But while by my father's poor hearth I wrought,
God filled me with many a holy thought."

"Set down your lantern and put out the light.
Here is gold : none can help you, 'tis dead of night."

"Good sirs ! for my brother the young priest's sake ;
If he heard such sayings his heart would break."

*   *   *   *   *

"Oh, plunge me down fathoms deep in the sea,
Of your mercy, rather than this thing be !

"Rather than this—'twere a lighter doom—
Oh bury me quick in a living tomb !"

*   *   *   *   *

The motherly hostess, sore afraid,
Waited in vain for her little maid.

She watched by the chill hearth's flickering light
Till the bell tolled twice through the black dead night.

Then cried, " Up, serving-men, sleep no more !

Help !—little maid Mignon lies drowned in gore."

*   *   *   *   *

By the cross she lay dead, in the dead cold night,

But beside her her lantern was still alight !

II.

THE FOSTER BROTHER.

Of all the noble damsels, in all our Brittany,

Gwennola was the sweetest far, a maiden fair to see.

Scarce eighteen summers shed their gold upon her
   shapely head,

Yet all who loved the fair girl best were numbered with
   the dead—

Her father and her mother, and eke her sisters dear.

Ah ! Mary, pity 'twas to see her shed the bitter tear

At her casement in the castle, where a step-dame now
  bare sway,
Her dim eyes fixed upon the sea, which glimmered far
  away.

*   *   *   *   *   *

For three long years she watched in vain, in dole and
  misery,
To see her foster brother's sail spring up from over sea ;

For three long years she watched in vain, hoping each
  day would send
The only heart which beat to hers, her lover and her
  friend.

"Go, get you gone and tend the kine," the cruel step-
  dame said ;
" Leave brooding over long-past years : go, earn your
  daily bread."

She woke her, ere the darkling dawns, while yet 'twas
dead of night,
To sweep the floors and cleanse the house, and set the
fires alight ;

To fetch the water from the brook, again and yet again,
With heavy toil and panting breath, and young form bent
in twain.

*　　　*　　　*　　　*　　　*　　　*

One darkling winter morning, before the dawning light,
With ringing hoofs, across the brook there rode a noble
knight :

"Good morrow, gracious maiden, and art thou free to
wed ? "
And she, so young she was and meek, "I know not, sir,"
she said.

" I prithee tell me, maiden, if thou art fancy-free?"
"To none, sir, have I plighted yet my maiden troth,"
said she.

"Then take, fair maid, this ring of gold, and to your
step-dame say,
That to-day your troth is plighted to a knight from far
away;

"That at Nantes a battle fierce was fought, wherein his
squire was slain,
And he himself lies stricken sore upon his bed of pain:

"But when three weeks are overpast, whatever fate betide,
He will come himself full gaily, and claim thee for his
bride."

All breathless ran she homeward, when, lo, a wondrous
thing!
For on her slender finger blazed her foster brother's ring.

II.

The weeks crept onward slowly, crept slowly—one, two,
  three;
But never came the young knight, no never more came he.

" Come, it is time that you were wed, for I have sought
  for you
A bridegroom fitted to your rank, an honest man and
  true."

" Nay, nay, I prithee, step-dame, there is none that I can
  wed,
Only my foster brother dear I love, alive or dead.

" With this ring his troth he plighted, and whatever fate
  betide,
He will come himself full gaily, and claim me for his
  bride."

" Peace, with thy golden wedding-ring ! peace, fool, or I
    will teach
With blows thy senseless chattering tongue to hold dis-
    creeter speech ;

"To-morrow thou shalt be the bride, whether thou wilt
    or not,
Of Giles the neat-herd, honest man : ay, this shall be thy
    lot."

"Of Giles the neat-herd, saidst thou? oh, I shall die of
    pain !
Oh mother, dear dead mother, that thou wert in life
    again ! "

"Go, cry and wail without the house; go, feed on misery;
Go, take thy fill of moans and tears, for wedded thou
    shalt be."

III.

Just then the ancient sexton, with the bell that tolls the
dead,
Went up and down the country side, and these the words
he said :—

" Pray for the soul of one who was a brave and loyal
knight,
Who bare at Nantes a grievous hurt, what time they
fought the fight :

" To-morrow eve, at set of sun, amid the gathering gloom,
From the white church they bear him forth, to rest within
the tomb."

IV.

" Thou art early from the wedding feast ! "   "Good truth,
  I could not stay ;
I dared not see the piteous sight, and therefore turned
  away ;

" I could not bear the pity and the horror in her eyne,
As she stood so fair, in blank despair, within the sacred
  shrine.

" Around the hapless maiden, all were weeping bitterly,
And the good old rector at the church, a heavy heart
  had he ;

"Not a dry eye was around her, save the step-dame stern
  alone,
Who looked on with an evil smile, as from a heart of
  stone ;

" And when the ringers rang a peal, as now they came
   again,
And the women whispered comfort, yet her heart seemed
   rent in twain.

" High in the place of honour at the marriage feast she
   sate,
Yet no drop of water drank she, and no crumb of bread
   she ate ;

" And when at last, the feast being done, they would light
   the bride to bed,
The ring from off her hand she flung, the wreath from off
   her head,

"And with wild eyes that spoke despair, and locks that
   streamed behind,
Into the darkling night she fled, as swiftly as the wind."

v.

The lights within the castle were out, and all asleep;
Only, with fever in her brain, the maid would watch and
    weep.

The chamber door swung open.   " Who goes there ? "
    " Do not fear,
Gwen ; 'tis I, your foster brother."   " Oh ! at last, my
    love, my dear ! "

He raised her to the saddle, and his strong arm clasped
    her round,
As, through the night, his charger white flew on without a
    sound.   '

" How fast we go, my brother ! "   " 'Tis a hundred
    leagues and more."
" How happy am I, happier than in all my life before !

"And have we far to go, brother ? I would that we were
come."

" Have patience, sister; hold me fast; 'tis a long way to
our home."

The white owl shrieked around them, the wild things
shrank in fear

As through the night a cloud of light that ghostly steed
drew near.

" How swift your charger is, brother ! and your armour,
oh, how bright !

Ah, no more you are a boy, brother, but in troth a noble
knight !

" How beautiful you are, brother ! but I would that we
were come."

" Have patience, sister ; hold me fast; we are not far
from home."

" Your breath is icy-cold, brother, your locks are dank
    and wet ;

Your heart, your hands are icy-cold; oh ! is it further
    yet ? "

" Have patience, sister ; hold me fast ; for we are nearly
    there

Hist ! hear you not our marriage bells ring through the
    midnight air ? "

Even with the word, that ghostly steed neighed suddenly
    and shrill,

Then trembled once through every limb, and like a stone
    stood still.

    *   *   *   *   *   *   *   *

And lo, within a land they were, a land of mirth and
    pleasure,

Where youths and maidens hand in hand danced to a
    joyous measure ;

A verdant orchard closed them round with golden fruit
  bedight,

And above them, from the heaven-kissed hills, came shafts
  of golden light ;

Hard by, a cool spring bubbled clear, a fountain without
  stain,

Whereof the dead lips tasting, grew warm with life again.

There was Gwennola's mother mild, and eke her sisters
  dear :

Oh, land of joy and bliss and love !—oh, land without
  a tear !

VI.

But when the next sun on the earth, brake from the
  gathered gloom,

From the white church, the young maids bore, the
  virgin to her tomb.

III.

AZENOR.

"Seamen, seamen, tell me true,
Is there any of your crew
Who in Armor town has seen
Azenor the kneeling queen?"

"We have seen her oft indeed,
Kneeling in the self-same place;
Brave her heart, though pale her face,
White her soul, though dark her weed."

I.

Of a long-past summer's day
Envoys came from far away,

Mailed in silver, clothed with gold,

On their snorting chargers bold.

When the warder spied them near,

To the King he went, and cried,

"Twelve bold knights come pricking here :

Shall I open to them wide?"

"Let the great gates opened be ;

See the knights are welcomed all ;

Spread the board and deck the hall

We will feast them royally."

"By our Prince's high command,

Who one day shall be our King,

We come to ask a precious thing—

Azenor your daughter's hand."

" Gladly will we grant your prayer :

Brave the youth, as we have heard.

Tall is she, milkwhite and fair,

Gentle as a singing bird."

Fourteen days high feast they made,

Fourteen days of dance and song ;

Till the dawn the harpers played ;

Mirth and joyance all day long.

" Now, my fair spouse, it is meet

That we turn us toward our home."

" As you will, my love, my sweet ;

Where you are, there I would come."

II.

When his step-dame saw the bride,
Well-nigh choked with spleen was she :
" This pale-faced girl, this lump of pride—
And shall she be preferred to me?

" New things please men best, 'tis true,
And the old are cast aside.
Natheless, what is old and tried
Serves far better than the new."

Scarce eight months had passed away
When she to the Prince would come,
And with subtlety would say,
" Would you lose both wife and home ?

" Have a care, lest what I tell

Should befall you ; so 'twere best

Have a care and guard you well,

'Ware the cuckoo in your nest."

" Madam, if the truth you tell,

Meet reward her crime shall earn,

First the round tower's straitest cell,

Then in nine days she shall burn."

III.

When the old King was aware,

Bitter tears the greybeard shed.

Tore in grief his white, white hair,

Crying, " Would God that I were dead

And to all the seamen said,

"Good seamen, pray you tell me true,

Is there, then, any one of you

Can tell me if my child be dead?"

" My liege, as yet alive is she,

Though burned to-morrow shall she be .

But from her prison tower, O King!

Morning and eve we hear her sing.

" Morning and eve, from her fair throat

Issues the same sweet plaintive note,

' They are deceived ; I kiss Thy rod :

Have pity on them, O my God !'"

IV.

Even as a lamb who gives its life
All meekly to the cruel knife,
White-robed she went, her soft feet bare,
Self-shrouded in her golden hair.

And as she to her dreadful fate
Fared on, poor innocent, meek and mild,
" Grave crime it were," cried small and great,
" To slay the mother and the child."

All wept sore, both small and great;
Only the step-dame smiling sate :
" Sure 'twere no evil deed, but good,
To kill the viper with her brood."

"Quick, good firemen, fan the fire
Till it leap forth fierce and red ;
Fan it fierce as my desire :
She shall burn till she is dead."

Vain their efforts, all in vain,
Though they fanned and fanned again ;
The more they blew, the embers gray
Faded and sank and died away.

When the judge the portent saw,
Dazed and sick with fear was he :
"She is a witch, she flouts the law ;
Come, let us drown her in the sea."

V

What saw you on the sea? A boat
Neither by sail nor oarsman sped ;
And at the helm, to watch it float,
An angel white with wings outspread ;

A little boat, far out to sea,
And with her child a fair ladye,
Whom at her breast she sheltered well,
Like a white dove upon a shell.

She kissed, and clasped, and kissed again
His little back, his little feet,
Crooning a soft and tender strain,
" Da-da, my dear ; da-da, my sweet.

" Ah, could your father see you, sweet,

A proud man should he be to-day ;

But we on earth may never meet,

But he is lost and far away."

VI.

In Armor town is such affright

As never castle knew before,

For at the midmost hour of night

The wicked step-dame is no more.

" I see hell open at my side :

Oh, save me, in God's name, my son !

Your spouse was chaste ; 'twas I who lied ;

Oh, save me, for I am undone ! "

Scarce had she checked her lying tongue,

When from her lips a snake did glide,

With threatening jaws, which hissed and stung,

And pierced her marrow till she died.

Eftsoons, to foreign realms the knight

Went forth, by land and over sea ;

Seeking in vain his lost delight,

O'er all the round, round world went he.

He sought her East, he sought her West,

Next to the hot South sped he forth,

Then, after many a fruitless quest,

He sought her in the gusty North.

There by some nameless island vast,

His anchor o'er the side he cast ;

When by a brooklet's fairy spray,

He spies a little lad at play.

Fair are his locks, and blue his eyes,

As his lost love's or as the sea ;

The good knight looking on them, sighs,

" Fair child, who may thy father be ? "

" Sir, I have none save Him in heaven :

Long years ago he went away,

Ere I was born, and I am seven ;

My mother mourns him night and day."

" Who is thy mother, child, and where ? "

" She cleanses linen white and fair,

In yon clear stream." " Come, child, and we

Together will thy mother see."

He took the youngling by the hand,

And, as they passed the yellow strand,

The child's swift blood in pulse and arm

Leapt to his father's and grew warm.

" Rise up and look, oh mother dear ;

It is my father who is here :

My father who was lost is come—

Oh, bless God for it !—to his home."

They knelt and blessed His holy name,

Who is so good, and just, and mild,

Who joins the sire and wife and child :

And so to Brittany they came.

And may the blessed Trinity,

Protect all toilers on the sea !

PRINTED BY WILLIAM CLOWES AND SONS, LIMITED, LONDON AND BECCLES.

www.ingramcontent.com/pod-product-compliance
Lightning Source LLC
Chambersburg PA
CBHW030819270326
41928CB00007B/812